Asteroids in the Birth Chart

Emma Belle Donath

ISBN: 0-86690-081-0

First Printing: 1979
Sixth Printing: 2003

Published by:
American Federation of Astrologers, Inc.
6535 S. Rural Road
Tempe, AZ 85283

Printed in the United States of America

"God grant that I may speak according to His will, and that my own thoughts may be worthy of His gifts; for even wisdom is under God's direction and He corrects the wise; we and our words, prudence, knowledge and craftsmanship, all are in His hand."—Wisdom of Solomon Chapter 6, v. 15-16 The New English Bible, Oxford Study Edition

Books By Emma Belle Donath

Approximate Positions of Asteroids, 1900-1999
Approximate Positions of Asteroids, 1851-2050
Asteroids in the Birth Chart
Asteroids in the Birth Chart
Asteroids in Midpoints, Aspects
and Planetary Pictures
Asteroids in Synastry
Asteroids in the U.S.A.
Have We Met Before?
Minor Aspects Between Natal Planets
Patterns of Professions
Relocation

Contents

Ceres

Habits - Nurturing

Pallas Athena

Patterns - Protecting

Juno

Ceremonies - Perpetuating

Vesta

Rituals - Preserving

Foreword

Asteroids—should they play a significant role in astrology? Astrologers have various viewpoints regarding asteroids and are not quite sure how they should fit in or even if they *should* fit in—and, so, why four for one sign? Some people swear by them; others feel perhaps it is no more important than a point on a chart, Vertex or Arabian point, but seems to be an enigma among many astrologers. Of course, there is the "Titius-Bode Law" showing that the asteroids should be located at 2.8 astronomical units from the sun. That theory certainly pinpointed their location and roughly that of Saturn and Uranus but not beyond this point. However, when examining the prime number of formalism devised by Dr. Astronomer Theodor Landscheidt we find:

Dr. Landschedit's later discovery shows there is a second generation of prime numbers consisting of the numbers 5, 7,11 and 19. He applied these four numbers to Venus, Earth, Mars and the Planetoids. The second group of prime numbers is applied to Jupiter and Saturn. The third group is applied to Uranus, Neptune, and Pluto. The fourth is applied to Transpluto. In using the subshells of prime numbers, the number 7 is analogous to the first group; two 7's to the second group; three 14's to the third group; and four 42's to the fourth group. The relationship is as an electron is to a subshell of an atom compared with the periodic system of chemical elements as relates to planetary groups. With these individual classifications, the seven periods of elements can be developed.[1]

I	II	III	IV
-♀⊕♂ P1	♃ ♄	Ψ	Tp
7	7 7	14 14 14	42
1	2 3	4 5 6	7

Figure I—Classification of Planetary Groups

The prime numbers as follows are assigned to each of the planets: Venus—5; Earth—7; Mars—11; Planetoids—19; Jupiter—37; Saturn—67; Uranus—137; Neptune—211; Pluto—283; and Transpluto—563. Earth is used as the astronomical unit one from the Sun. Divide 7 into, for example, the number for Mars. The result would be 1.5. Similarly, in dividing 7 (Earth) into 211 (Neptune) the result would be 30.1—the approximate location of Neptune today in astronomical units. (Hawkins, 1976, pp. 11-12).

	♀	⊕	♂	P1	♃	♄		Ψ		Tp
Titius-Bode	0,7	1	1,6	2,8	5,2	10	19,6	38,8	77,2	154
observed:	0,7	1	1,5	2,8	5,2	9,5	19,2	30,1	39,8*	(77-80)
number sequence:	0,7	1	1,5	2,7	5,2	9,5	19,3	29,9**	40,0	79,5

*Author's correction: 39,4 **Author's correction: 30,1

Figure 2—Planetary Distance (A.U.) by Prime Numbers

[1] John Robert Hawkins, M.S. *Transpluto or Should We Call Him BACCHUS The Ruler of Taurus?* (Dallas, 1976), pp. 11-12.

Taking the sum of these prime numbers (1340) and applying the dimensionless number 1836.12 (the relationship between the masses of proton and electron) using the Fine Structure Constant (137.032), we find 1340 is the total of prime numbers since the precise ratio of the abstract number in physics collapses on the number of further rational numbers to the sum rn. The factor is 10^2.

Looking at this, we find the planets are located very close—clear out to Transpluto (Bacchus) where they should be today. This is very significant and further reading in Dr. Landscheidt's book, *Cosmic Cybernetics,* relates these different chemical periodical groups related to different planets. Thus, by "Titius-Bode Law" and Prime Number formalism at 2.8 A.U., a planetary body should be represented.

In mythology, it is also very significant when looking at the planets themselves, the different gods and goddesses, and how they apply in today's world. We find there are only certain planets named from a certain group of gods and goddesses. Mythology has given the key. Neptune rules the twelfth house (the sign of Pisces) which holds the secrets and the mysteries.

Greek mythology begins with Uranus (heaven) and Gaea (earth), the parents of the Titans—six brothers and six sisters. The Titans, incited by Gaea, overthrew Uranus and made Saturn (Chronos), their younger brother, the ruler. Chronos married his sister, Rhea, and from this union came six major Greek Gods: Zeus, Hera, Hades, Poseidon, Demeter, and

Hestia. Zeus, after dethroning Chronos, became the father of all the other great gods and goddesses—Athena, Apollo, Artemis, Ares, Hepaestus, Hermes, Dionysus and Aphrodite. All of these are in the Olympian group and all the planets in our solar system thus far named are from these gods and goddesses. With the rise of Rome, the Greek names were replaced by Roman ones. Thus, Hestia became Vesta; Demeter, Ceres; Hera, Juno; Poseidon, Neptune, etc. Within this group, all the gods and goddesses have rulership power over certain signs of the zodiac. But, two signs remain unnamed—without a god or goddess. Uranus rules Aquarius; Saturn rules Capricorn; Neptune rules Pisces. Pluto was not named within this group because he was god of the underworld and thus was not on Mt. Olympus; however, he rules Scorpio. Jupiter rules Sagittarius; Hermes or Mercury rules Gemini; Apollo, the Sun, rules Leo; Artemis or Diana, the Moon, rules Cancer; Ares or Mars rules Aries; and Aphrodite or Venus rules Libra. Only two signs remain unnamed—Taurus and Virgo. The mythological meanings of Vesta, Ceres, Juno and Athena (for Minerva or Pallas) have to do more with Virgo (Hawkins, 1976, p.16).

Firstly, there were two great Earth gods—one called Bacchus, known as both the wine and bull god, and the other Demeter (or Ceres) the goddess of corn or small grains.[2] Bac-

---

[2] Edith Hamilton, *Mythology.* (New American Library, New York, 1969), p. 47.

chus was also called Taurus, the bull god.[3] The constellation Virgo represents a woman with a branch in her right hand and some ears of corn in her left. The Hebrew name for Virgo is "a virgin." The constellation of Virgo itself describes her as a woman with ears of corn.[4] Further, this is stated: "the Terrestial Virgin Mother is Ceres, or Demeter, and Virgo is identified with her . . . Virgin Mother of World Saviors . . . Ceres, Myrrha, Mary . . . were inducted into the Virgin mysteries or Madonna Rites under the Virgo Hierarchy. . . ."[5] This is what Ceres or Demeter, in Greek and Roman mythology was—the goddess of corn. Could anything be clearer than that the constellation itself assigns Ceres as goddess of Virgo!

Demeter (Ceres) was known as the great mother goddess, as known in the Eleusian mysteries which originated the virgin mother (virgin Mary) and the child theme. This was represented by the accompanying North Constellation of Virgo, known as Coma (woman and child). We find when her daughter, Kore or Persephone, was lost, or kidnapped by Pluto, she would not let any fruit or grain grow on Earth, causing famine until she recovered her daughter. She symbolizes what one really cares for or about. Pallas, the next significant goddess, was a goddess of understanding. She was very skilled in handicrafts and was called the mistress of

[3] Robert Graves, *The Greek Myths: J.* (Penguin Books, Baltimore, Maryland, 1960), p. 296.

[4] Howard B. Rand, *The Stars Declare God's Handiwork.* (Merrimac, Mass., 1944), pp. 2-3.

[5] Corinne Heline, *Mythology and the Bible.* (New Age Press, Inc. La Canada, Calif., 1972), p. 23.

industry. The ancient name for the accompanying constellation (Coma) of Virgo, meant desired or the longed for . . . the identical word for the Holy Spirit in Hag 2:7.[6] The Holy Spirit in the Bible is symbolized by olive oil and means light, understanding and wisdom. The parable of the ten virgins shows only five virgins were wise and had oil in their lamps. It is significant because Pallas was called the goddess of wisdom, also symbolized by the olive tree and represents analyzing the parts and putting them together to make a whole. Pallas is what you know and understand.

The first two asteroids are located and rotate at 2.767 A.U. and 4.6012 sidereal years; and 2.772 A.U. and 4.6069 sidereal years, respectively. Both are closest to the prime number formalism and the "Titius-Bode Law" and were the first two discovered of the asteroids. Ceres, the largest, was discovered New Year's Day, 1801. and Pallas, March 28, 1802. These two planetoids play a major role in the sign of Virgo. Then the planetoid Juno, wife of Jupiter, was discovered September 1, 1804, and Vesta, the vestal virgin, followed on March 29, 1807.

Another accompanying North constellation of Virgo is Bootes (the Coming One). In addition to the reaper pictured by the sickle it means to tread underfoot, anger and vengeance. (Rand, 1944, p. 3). Juno depicted this with her fits of jealousy, anger and vengeance she reaped on those involved with her husband Jupiter. Juno represents critical ability. Vesta, the vestal virgin, kept the fires and offered sacrifices

[6]Rand, p.3

of the fruits or harvest and meal offerings—these were sin offerings and in particular represented healing of the body. She was the purest of all (asteroid Vesta is the only asteroid unmarked and unpotted), and is represented by the other accompanying constellation South of Virgo, known as Asmeath, meaning sin-offering or making one's soul as an offering for sin. (Rand, 1944, p. 3). This is why Vesta represents a job or duty that is dull and boring to the point that it becomes a sacrifice. Vesta also equates to security; the constellation and accompanying constellations of Virgo itself tell its rulers by their meanings. What could be plainer than the constellation itself! God challenged Job: "Canst Thou bring forth the Mazzorth (the twelve signs of the Zodiac or constellations of the Zodiac) in his season?" Job 38:32. The Hebrews knew the original meanings of the constellations. This divine knowledge was preserved by them. Will one argue with the Maker of the Heavens?

It is very interesting that it took another 38 years before the next asteroid was discovered. Could it not be that the heavens themselves were telling us these four planetoids would play the major role in the asteroid belt—the four being virgins as represented by the name Virgo? No wonder, these were the only four goddesses left on Mt. Olympus. Why should there be four planetoids ruling the sign of Virgo and not just one? This is very intriguing to most. Let's examine: First, the concept of Virgo means to serve. If there were one rulership, one would be served, rather than serving—losing the complete meaning of Virgo. It is the mass (the working classes) serving the one big boss. Therefore, the rulership of Virgo must be made up of more than one ruler in Virgo. The working class of people are told what to do. That is why in the asteroid belt, the planets Mars and Jupiter influence the rotational movement of the asteroids, without complete freedom on their own, and to a certain degree are more or less told what to do, unlike planets which rule their own signs.

The next question is why the number four? The number four is a basic number. The Empedoclean concept is four elements: fire, air, water and earth. In Heitzenberg's universal formula, he is convinced that in all elementary processes, from which all natural phenomena evolve, four different groups are to be distinguished. Along with this we find that there are four classes of elementary particles, namely the photon group, the leptons,and mesons and the baryons. In addition, Dirac Friedemann, and Eddington endeavor to devise structural models comprehensively reflecting natural phenomena, all used four basic elements as a starting point.[7] Also, we find in the prime number formalism used there were four elements consisting of 5, 7, 11 and 19. It is extremely interesting because it is a foundation or a basis. Perhaps what is more interesting and important is the digestive system which Virgo represents.

Of the asteroids, Ceres is the largest and when asteroids get larger in number generally they get smaller in size. It is believed that there are up to 200,000 asteroids, and all of them have not yet been found. This is certainly indicative in defining Virgo when it comes to numbers and details as they get smaller and smaller, much like the digestive system and

[7]Theodor Landscheidt, *Cosmic Cybernetics The Foundations of a Modern, Astrology,* (Federal Republic of Germany, 1973), pp. 26-27.

the way food is brought in (which is Ceres, the gatherer) and then is continually broken down until digested. Further in the digestive system, there are four major parts: first the mouth and saliva which brings in the large particles of food by being analyzed and critically examined as to where it should be broken down; the small intestine, where food is broken down and digested; and finally, the large intestine, the end result of what is pure and what is to be eliminated in waste. Notice that the large food particles are broken down smaller and smaller, the same as the asteroid belt. The stomach of a herbivorous animal has four parts that determine where different food particles should go. There are four enzymes in the digestive system—one breaks down proteins, one starches, one fats, and one sugars—four as a whole. It should be clear that there are four planetoids/asteroids which make up the sign of Virgo. Additionally, there are only four virgins left of the Olympian goddesses, all of which had mythological meanings pertaining to the sign of Virgo. Ceres, the goddess of grain and the great gatherer, had to do with the agricultural industry. Pallas, the mistress of industry, pertains to the non-agricultural industry. These two goddesses serve the two major industries. Juno, the wife of Jupiter who took her virginal rites yearly to remain a virgin, portrays serving in a marital state. Vesta, the vestal virgin, portrays serving in an unmarried state. Service is the real meaning behind Virgo.

Examining the different services each asteroid provides, one learns in detail how service is to really be performed. It is no small wonder Christ got angry at some of his disciples when they were trying to determine who would sit on His right hand. Then, Christ said, "let him that would be the greatest among you be the servant of all". In other words, the greatest master is the greatest servant of all, or he who serves the most. This is what Virgo teaches in great detail.

How significant are the asteroids within one's chart? Looking at the asteroids, we deal with details and finer points within a chart, naturally. Some people say this is a lot of work. This is true because that is exactly what Virgo represents—a lot of work and a lot of service. If you are going to get down to real details in a chart, then you bring these in. It is obvious the four asteroids have a great deal of power even though their relative size is small. One realizes that the power of planets come not from size or distance from the sun, but by its material content as witnessed by Pluto, small in size and yet farthest from the sun.

In the past there has been a significant amount of work done regarding asteroids, both by Eleanor Bach and Zipporah Pottenger Dobyns, PhD., but no one until now has put it all together. Now, Emma Belle Donath has done just that. We have not only an ephemeris, but the planets in signs, in houses, aspects to each other, and midpoints. This is a major undertaking to be completed on any subject in astrology, let along the sign of Virgo. This series goes a long way to answer many questions. Naturally continual research needs to be done to keep the material updated. This series of books, however, is a major foundation on which to build future knowledge.

John Robert Hawkins, M.S.

Preface to the First Edition

It was a search for the ruler of Virgo that led to my work with the major asteroids. Being a Gemini, I refused to share Mercury with another. After trying several other suggestions, I began using the asteroids Ceres, Pallas Athena, Juno and Vesta in my research and found some results which are being shared with you in this volume.

There are several theories concerning this grouping of small planets or particles between Mars and Jupiter. According to Bode's law of physics there should be a planet in this region. Some astronomers and astrologers believe the gases in the area simply did not adhere together in a denser mass but cooled into small atmosphereless rocks. Other theories include the possibility of a planet which exploded from external or internal pressures. Many articles have been written about this imaginary planet called Rex by esotericists. Mention of it is made in Taylor Caldwell's novel *Dialogues With the Devil.* Regardless of their origin these bodies do exist and can be both seen and tracked.

In working with Ceres, Pallas Athena, Juno and Vesta there is predominantly a concern with relationships. Not the true equal partnerships of the coming Aquarius-Leo Age but the employer-employee, server-receiver relations of our present Pisces-Virgo Age. We find aspects to one or more of these four asteroids in both the coming into and the going out of relationships.

This book is certainly not a final source but only some results of personal research which hopefully will encourage each of you to use these asteroids in your own work. It is only by experimenting and comparing ideas that we gain new information in all scientific fields, including astrology.

Particular thanks and acknowledgment is given to the following people for their help. Dr. Elisabeth V. Bacon and astrologer Carol Jaramillo, both of Columbus, Ohio, for their cooperation in this work; my husband Robert C. Donath for his encouragement; my friend Marilyn Hoffman for her assistance; my teacher Audreana Ades of Cincinnati, Ohio, for instructing me in the exciting study of astrology over the years; and to the many friends and students who shared their charts to make this research possible.

Books which were of particular help included *Planets and Asteroids, Relationships in Conjunctions,* by Esther V. Leinbach; *Ephemerides of the Asteroids, Ceres, Pallas, Juno and Vesta, 1900-2000,* by Eleanor Bach; *The Asteroids,* by Alan E. Nourse; and *Greek Mythology,* by Paul Hamlyn. Articles and workshops by Dr. Zipporah Dobyns and Laura Ruben have added much information to this study.

Emma Belle Donath, February 1976

Preface to the Second Edition

In reprinting *Asteroids in the Birth Chart* it seems only fitting to share data collected over the past years. Comments and correspondence received concerning these first basic interpretations have been overwhelming. Out of over 2000 responses only three persons found any variances with the simple meanings printed in 1976. Of course, as astrologers work more closely with Ceres, Pallas Athena, Juno and Vesta the delineations presented in this primer will be expanded and refined a hundredfold.

Research is presently in progress analyzing biological and medical interpretations, intelligence potential, mundane delineations and midpoint results with the asteroids. Relationship data have been reported in my book *Asteroids in Synastry*. Esther V. Leinbach completed her comprehensive volume *Transits*. It deals with the transiting effects of these four asteroids over both the traditional planets and the asteroids in each zodiacal sign. Esther has again provided us with a sensitive and accurate astrological insight into our world.

John R. Hawkins of Dallas, Texas, has graciously written an enlightening foreword about the asteroids for this revised book. When I first met John we found that we shared more than merely the same degrees on our Midheavens and Ascendants; we were both actively engaged in researching relatively unknown planetary bodies. John has authored and published a comprehensive book, *Transpluto, or Should We Call Him Bacchus, The Ruler of Taurus?*. In addition he has researched the use of the four major asteroids in both natal and mundane astrology. An Aquarian, John is a practitioner of both traditional astrology and cosmobiology. He has an M.S. in Agriculature from East Texas State University, a B.S. in Theology and post graduate studies from Ambassador College, as well as credentials from Purdue University. A member of numerous astrological organizations, he has spoken and written prolifically. I am very grateful for the mythological, astrological and astronomical understanding which he has shared in this foreword.

An Appendix on astronomical characteristics of the asteroid belt has been added to this edition to aid comprehension of the physical laws of this portion of space. Astrological interpretation must be synonymous with existing universal rules. It behooves all who are involved in research to be cognizant of present scientific findings as well as past facts and theories. Discovery of the planetary body Chiron in late fall of 1977 has been under constant investigation by alert astrologers and astronomers who are adding daily information to accumulated knowledge. This new body may be pertinent to our consideration of the known asteroid belt as suggested by astronomer George Wallerstein of the University of Washington. In a discussion of similarities between Ohiron and Pluto he theorized that there may be a large class of such objects with Pluto being the largest and Chiron the nearest. Mr. Wallerstein further noted in his letter to *Sky and Telescope* magazine, March 1978, that another vast number of asteroids may await discovery outside the orbit of Neptune.

Last year Asteroid 4 or Vesta passed its perihelion point on June 5, 1978, and was closer to the Sun than at any period since June of 1949. With this event I expected some additional astrological information about Vesta. Later in the summer, at the American Federation of Astrologers' Conference in Atlanta, Georgia, an excellent research study was presented in book form, *Sexual Assaults: Pro-Identifying Those Vulnerable*, by T. Patrick Davis. Since it has long been my policy to add the asteroids to any valid astrological study I placed them in Ms. Davis's charts. The asteroid Vesta figured prominently into the investigation. Vesta, which can represent sexual perversion as well as chastity, was involved in every case of assault repored. By progression, direction or transit this asteroid was connected to the Chain-Reaction Pattern of each victim. It was also involved with the natal Chain-Reaction Patterns. Where the assault was the first sexual experience, Juno, biologically representing the hymen, was involved in the Pattern. Vesta combined with Saturn in most of the charts where the victims were also murdered, giving violent denial of life.

I have in my possession six sources giving the positions for the four major asteroids. To the best of my ability I have used those positions which seem to be the most accurate from my current research. All charts in this book have been brought up to date where indicated. Precise positions of

Ceres, Pallas Athena, Juno and Vesta are included in Appendix B. Appendix B positions are from Astro-Computing Services, PO Box 16297, San Diego, California 92116, and are printed with permission. ACS preferred that the exact positions be given rather than rounded off to degrees as in *Approximate Positions of the Asteroids, 1900-1999.* Instructions are given in the Appendix to permit calculations of the approximate positions of the major asteroids. For daily positions, plus declinations, researchers are urged to consult *The Asteroid Ephemeris, 1883-1999* by Dr. Zipporah P. Dobyns, Rique Pottenger and Neil Michelsen, TIA Publications 1977. Sign relativity tables for these asteroids are given in *Asteroids in the U.S.A.* along with percentage of retrograde occurrence and out-of-bounds declination tables.

Future placements of Ceres, Pallas Athena, Juno and Vesta are given for the years 2001 through 2050 in Appendix D. They are being printed only because I enjoy exploring the unknown and the uncharted and hope that others may join me in these flights into the future. Appendix D. monthly positions were programmed by Wilayne Clawson of Romulus, Michigan, on her Commodore PET home computer system. With high perturbations of the asteroids, especially Pallas Athena and Juno, there may later be found differences for this time span.

Over the past years several national magazines have begun to publish articles about the asteroids, either natally or by transit. *Stellium Quarterly* has printed research reports about the asteroids from numerous contributors. *Phenomena* presents the latest scientific findings and *Starcraft Horoscope* has a regular column on effects of the transiting asteroids for the various Sun Signs. In the October 1978, issue, *Astrology Now* magazine graciously printed some of my recent data concerning these little planets. Local astrological associations are gathering material from study and use of the asteroids in Atlanta, Chicago, El Paso, Dallas-Fort Worth, Baltimore, New York and other cities.

I extend a very special "thank you" to Arlene Kramer, Noel Tyl and Kt Boehrer, who have kindly consented to allow me to present their comments about *Asteroids in the Birth Chart* on the back cover of this revised edition of the book. They have each been supportive and helpful in promoting the use of these planetoids throughout the astrological community. It was especially nice for them to befriend me in my initial attempt as an author. Thank you all three again for your patience, guidance and encouragement.

Emma Belle Donath, April 1979

Chapter 1

Ceres

Worship of Ceres, Goddess of the Harvest, dates back to Etruscan times if not earlier. This lovely, flaxen-haired maiden was known as Demeter by the Greeks. When the Festival of Cerelia was adopted by the Romans, Demeter was renamed Ceres and added to their family of gods. Legends about her include the well-known search for her daughter Persephone in the underworld and the gift of seeds to the kings of earth. She was supposed to have brought the cultivation of grains to the land. Many of the keywords used in this book are derived from ancient legends.

This largest of the asteroids has as its main purpose domestication. As the ancient goddess taught men to cultivate the fertile soil, Ceres teaches discipline necessary for people to live together. This is the principle of nurturing and growing into the environment in which we were born.

Because we are dealing with early care and training there is a minute distinction. The mother principle, or Moon, bears and feeds the child in a very personal and emotional manner. Mercury, the early teacher, gives it skills of reading and writing to communicate with others. We need someone to train the child to live with people in the daily world. This teacher is best personified by the term British "nanny." She takes the little one and teaches it habits necessary for relationships. These lessons include toilet training, proper eating habits and elementary etiquette. When considered on a larger scale this leads to a true balance between man and nature or what we now call ecology.

Nursing is an enlargement upon the nurturing concept of Ceres. Here we find care of the physical body, not only of children but of the incapacitated of all ages. This is truly mother love on a universal scale. There is a necessity for emotional detachment so that the nurse may give injections, change bandages or cleanse wounds knowing that momentary pain is for the greater benefit. Such action shows an overview of the situation.

In selecting the dolphin, dove and ant to represent

Ceres we find creatures that work together in social units. Recall the sophisticated patterns of industrious ants working in their colonies. From present research with dolphins or porpoises we are learning that they can be easily trained to communicate with men. Ancient legends tell of these water animals even rescuing shipwrecked people and playing with them in the water.

Associating Ceres with Virgo gives a deeper understanding of these practical earth people. Like the planet on which we live there is a throbbing life beneath the seemingly placid surface. There is also a similarity between the seasonal patterns and effective use of resources by the earth and the organizational ability and efficiency of Virgo natives.

Keywords are given positively. Remember that aspects and transits may bring out the negative.

φ

Ceres—Goddess of the Harvest

Animal: Dolphin, pigs

Bird: Dove, crane

Insect: Ant

Plant: Cereal grains, corn, poppies

Emblem: Scythe, Torch, Sacrificial Knife

Principle: Nurturing, healing

Expression: Cultivation, harvest, domestication, nourishment, useful labor, austere beauty, instinctive racial feelings, heritage of primitive experience, initiator of future life, server, concern

Manifestation: Ecology, cereal grains, farm tools, toilet training, domestic animals and pets, harvest fairs, honey, bread, caves, underground water or springs

Personification: Nanny, servant, nurse, nursery school director, Earth science teacher, farmer, salutary laws, grandparent, grandchild

4

Ceres in the Signs

Ceres in Aries

Ceres in Aries means active harvest. These natives can be called do-gooders because they are overly eager to be helpful. There is a conflict between masculine drive and feminine gentleness causing them to seem constantly busy. They quite often tire before completing their planned projects. Concerned with results, they may be termed goal oriented.

Ceres in Taurus

Ceres in Taurus desires to grow living things. These are people with beautiful, natural physical bodies who have no problems with sex. There is a soothing grace of movement making them pleasant to be around. With strong fertility urges these people sometimes grow herbs on their windowsills or have plots in the community gardens. They may raise health gardens. They may raise health foods for money.

Ceres in Gemini

Ceres in Gemini gives a thoughtfulness concerning the life sustaining acts. These are people who talk about ecology and health foods. They adhere to the theory of live and let live so there is no aggression in this placement. Natural teachers, they sometimes work with retarded children and youth. They are quick to lend a helping hand to friend and neighbor alike.

Ceres in Cancer

Ceres in Cancer tends to care for people and animals efficiently. They may seem impersonal as mothers because of the blending of emotions and mental expression. They would prefer to train and teach rather than to cuddle and smother. This is a practical expression of domestic concerns which relieves the moodiness of Cancer.

Ceres in Leo

Ceres in Leo gives a strong life support system with a natural creative energy. Both a love and respect of children and nature is found. There is also the ability to work creatively with the hands in such fields as gardening, weaving and pottery. Here are our life squad volunteers, PTA workers and ecology promoters.

Ceres in Virgo

Ceres in Virgo likes to nurse people. The nurturers of the world, they give of their own energies to revitalize and restore people who come into their sphere of contact. Being interested in nutrition they care for the body properly. Here is growth without waste.

Ceres in Libra

Ceres in Libra prefers to be fair and truthful in dealing with people at all times. They are reliable and dependable in relations with others and like for all to share benefits equally. Here youwill find people who are concerned with equal employment opportunities. They judge according to their own concepts of what is fair.

Ceres in Scorpio

Ceres in Scorpio ignores setbacks and defeats while continuing on toward their goals. There is regenerative power in times of ill health. Psychic ability may be present without training.

Ceres in Sagittarius

Ceres in Sagittarius enjoys mental speculation about various theories and ideas. A natural sense of freedom combined with genuine optimism may cause these natives to overextend themselves. In every case so far investigated this placement has had periods of uncontrolled growth such as warts, tumors and cysts which were benign but had to be removed surgically.

Ceres in Capricorn

Ceres in Capricorn is a blending of the maternal and paternal principles into a workable combination. Learning is a pleasurable experience for these natives who are disciplined more effectively with rewards than with punishments. Because Ceres in this sign softens the soul's testing the person is encouraged to continued effort by defeat. This is a good bridge for communication and teaching as well as natural leadership.

Ceres in Aquarius

Ceres in Aquarius can humor other people into doing jobs for which they are best adapted. This placement brings tact and the ability to compromise, making them well liked by all.

Ceres in Pisces

Ceres in Pisces tends to narrow philosophical and religious issues to the core of their meaning and then to apply those principles to their everyday lives. They distill the essence of information given to them. Intuition is used in a practical way and all experiences are analyzed impersonally. This may eso-terically be called the sorrow before the spring.

Ceres in the Houses

Ceres in the First House

Ceres in the first house gives a natural grace in dress without excessive adornment. Good taste, modesty and stability are evident in appearances rather than extreme flair in clothes. Many of these people wear their hair in natural styles and use very little makeup. With Ceres rising or angular we often find people who are dedicated to caring for the home.

Ceres in the Second House

Ceres in the second house uses resources efficiently. This flow of creativity may range from a houseful of flowers in Taurus, care of children in Leo, or growth of money and prestige in Capricorn. They are always concerned with the steady growth of resources including money. Placed here Ceres gives a grace to the body movements which can soothe and heal other people.

Ceres in the Third House

Ceres in the third house makes people think and talk about the natural functions of life. In dealing with neighbors, close friends and relatives they believe in letting everyone have their own moral standards. These people are good at such things as organizing neighborhood picnics. A concern for children of the mind as well as of the body is evidenced here. These natives talk to their plants and small pets.

Ceres in the Fourth House

Ceres in the fourth house prefers natural wood tones in decorating. When preparing meals they will consider nutritional value and balance of the menu as well as the gourmet appeal. There is a balancing of feeling and communications. Home may be used as the base of operations or the work area.

Ceres in the Fifth House

Ceres in the fifth house brings the ability to heal and sooth. Fertility may also be indicated by aspects to Ceres. They might adopt children. Natives of this placement enjoy long walks in the country or out-of-doors where they can watch the birds and animals. They are not usually gamblers or speculators.

Ceres in the Sixth House

Ceres in the sixth house combines an interest in nutrition with concern for the body and the well-being of fellow workers. Living in a natural setting aids mental and emotional health for these natives. If they cannot live in the country, they need trees and flowers around the apartment or house. These are the people who clean up debris from the office party or see that the office is ready for the next day's work. They accept the routine details in office or plant. Look under keywords for more specific indications of job application.

Ceres in the Seventh House

Ceres in the seventh house likes to see the realistic balance in relationships. They recognize the value of being generous and expect others to do the same in a quiet, unassuming manner. Reliable and helpful, they are aroused to action by the underdog in any situation. Often they nurse their mates through serious illnesses.

10

Ceres in the Eighth House

Ceres in the eighth house brings a natural interest in the reproductive processes on the physical plane and a curiosity about reincarnation on the esoteric level. Natural foods are restorative in times of ill health and proper nutrition can prevent illness. Study of biological sciences or work in that field has been found here in every case compiled.

Ceres in the Ninth House

Ceres in the ninth house uses philosophical ideas in a practical and useful way. Higher education is undertaken for career advancement. They may camp, hike or bike across country.

Ceres in the Tenth House

Ceres in the tenth house is the organized executive. This is the dependable worker who gained prestige or advancement through hard and diligent work.

Ceres in the Eleventh House

Ceres in the eleventh house adds respectability to New Age activities as well as bringing together groups of people for humanitarian causes. Ceres tones down the desire to be controversial or shocking. They ease co-workers into the proper slots.

Ceres in the Twelfth House

Ceres in the twelfth house keeps the feet on the ground in religious endeavors. The intuitive ability is strong but useful rather than mystical. They live their beliefs. These natives may be found serving or nursing in hospitals or institutions. Ceres here protects against being hospitalized for mental or emotional illness.

Ceres Examples

The native described in Chart 1 brings out the traits of Ceres and Pallas by sign and house position so well that we will discuss them together. In 1956, this British nurse joined the Flying Nurses in Australia when Mars was transiting her natal Ceres and Pallas, followed later in the year by Saturn transits in Sagittarius. At the same time, transiting Ceres and Pallas were in Pisces squaring their natal positions, with Juno and Vesta transiting in Sagittarius. When she returned to England in 1960, via Bali and India, we found transits of Jupiter, Mars, Juno and Vesta in Sagittarius with Ceres and Pallas again in Pisces. The next time Ceres and Pallas were in Pisces our nurse accepted a position in a Canadian hospital. During this period in 1965, Mars and Juno in Sagittarius were squaring Saturn in Pisces as well as Uranus and Pluto in Virgo. The 1975 return of Ceres and Pallas to Pisces found her returning to England. At that time Neptune was transiting her Pallas and Vesta was in Pisces. During the 1970 transits of Ceres and Pallas in Pisces no

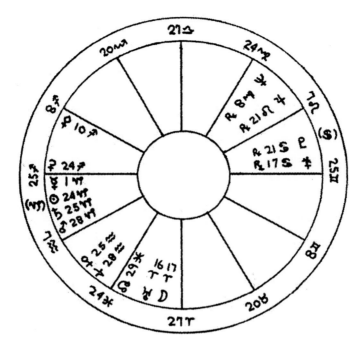

Chart 1   Female, January 15, 1932, Tropical Placidus

other planets were forming aspects in her chart. The squares trigger changes for her.

Here is a person who fulfills one personification of Ceres—nurse. She also has traveled all over the world working in institutions of suffering, suggested by both Ceres and Pallas in the twelfth house. With Pallas in Sagittarius she has traveled widely in her career.

To further substantiate the position of Ceres in Sagittarius this native had cysts removed surgically from ovaries and uterus while Mars was conjunct and Jupiter was squaring Ceres. All women researched with this Ceres placement reported periods of benign growths on the female organs.

This person also exemplifies the position with her curiosity about various religions and philosophies. Currently interested in I Ching, she is also taking a psychology course and reading about reincarnation. Also, true to her Pallas in the twelfth house, she becomes mentally interested but remains emotionally aloof from these diverse beliefs.

Chart 2 deals with Ceres in the eleventh house. This native owns and operates an astrology and occult bookstore and school. In addition she has started a successful book distribution center in the same midwestern city, pioneering in this field as indicated by Ceres in Aries.

She handles her business affairs in a very capable and traditional manner thus bringing respectability to this new type of venture. At no time does she impress people as controversial or shocking, despite her Sun in Aquarius.

In keeping with this placement, our native likes to work with groups and classes having recently sponsored

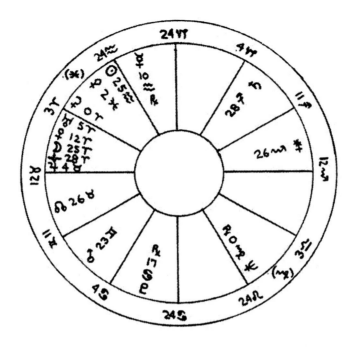

Chart 2 Female, February 14, 1929, Tropical Koch

a weekend of workshops attended by people from several states. She is always looking for new books and ideas to promote.

Ceres, Goddess of the Harvest
Esoteric Keywords

Chakra: Thyroid/Telepathy

Colors: Green and gold

Direction: West

Element: Earth

Energy: Healing through stones and gems

Number: 49, Search for perfection (higher octave of 7)

Ray: III, Intelligent activity

Symbol: Triangle around a circle

Esoteric keywords for the asteroids were derived by
Dr. Elizabeth Valentine Bacon of Columbus, Ohio,
and are printed with her permission.

Chapter 2

Pallas Athena

Pallas Athena, Goddess of Wisdom, was the divine child of Jupiter or Zeus who sprang fully grown from her father's forehead without benefit of a mother. And, like its namesake, the asteroid Pallas orbits closer to Jupiter than any other major asteroid. According to legend, the request of Pallas to remain a virgin was granted by Zeus. Therefore, her heart was reputed to remain insensitive to the pangs of love so that she was ruled by mind not emotions. We find that Pallas in the horoscope deals primarily with mental activities.

This goddess also became known as the protector of cities. In addition to teaching men to train horses and domesticate oxen, she taught them to defend and protect their cities and villages. Pallas Athena gave men the skills necessary to live profitably together and was known as the patron of architects, sculptors, spinners and weavers. She brought beauty and pattern into their lives.

As the social unit increased from family to tribe to city there was additional need for wise handling of issues. Pallas came to be considered the intercessor between the people and the government, thereby personifying the power of the intellect. A contemporary title for her would be ombudswoman.

Keywords, taken from ancient legends, show similar traits when tested in natal charts. For example, Pallas showed valour and cunning in time of war.

Her eternal virginity epitomizes the concept of modesty. She is associated with invention and skill because of the new ideas given men for easier and more pleasant living. Handcraft skills were evident in weaving, embroidery and spinning. There is certainly a perseverance connected with Pallas, but it is not severe or harsh.

In many of the charts, Pallas was concerned with career, particularly of women. One young woman with Pallas in Capricorn in her tenth house runs her own hardware store; another with Pallas in Gemini in the sixth house teaches retarded children; many with Pallas in the fourth house work in the home. It seems not so much to define the type of work as to explain the choice of career.

Symbols given for Pallas Athena are those traditionally mentioned with wisdom, such as the owl and the olive tree; the scarab is an ancient Egyptian symbol for wisdom. The unicorn, a mythical creature, brings beauty and a hint of idealism. Her diamond or shield was both ornamental and protective. If there seems to be a conflict in defining Pallas, remember that she was both builder and protector of the city. This must involve the principle of one who fights for peace and freedom as well as one who creates and develops.

Pallas Athena, Goddess of Wisdom

Animal: Unicorn

Bird: Owl, cock

Insect: Beetle or scarab

Plant: Olive tree, iris diamond or shield, lance

Principle: Prudent Intelligence, Intuition

Expression: Conservation, personification of light, invention, modesty, peacemaking, bravery, liaison, Insensitive to emotions, noble mind, perseverance, equality in work, cunning, skillful hands, valour, perception

Manifestation: Embroidery, weaving, job, flute, battle armour, industry, numbers, spinning, handcrafts, fulcrum point

Personification: Weaver, warrior for peace, crusader, patron of arts/crafts, working women, counselor, horse trainer, sculptor, librarian, vocational teacher, National Guardsman, ombudsman

Pallas Athena in the Signs

Pallas Athena in Aries

Pallas Athena in Aries brings the desire to start more projects than the native can physically complete. This cuts down on the efficiency of Pallas as well as causing frustration. A drive to pioneer, especially in the creation of new and unusual hand-crafts, leads these people into innovative hobbies and careers. There may be enough mental pressure to cause strain.

Pallas Athena in Taurus

Pallas Athena in Taurus indicates a great deal of artistic talent. There is special joy for these natives in recycling materials for their projects, such as piece-work quilting or braiding rag rugs from used wool. A balance of color and design is found in this placement. Such talents could be used in interior decorating or designing.

Pallas Athena in Gemini

Pallas Athena in Gemini is an optimistic placement and can give an excellent business mind. Many teachers and lecturers have this combination. One person with Pallas here prepares and demonstrates audio-visual aides for teachers to use in the classroom. There is usually extreme mental perception.

Pallas Athena in Cancer

Pallas Athena in Cancer analyzes feelings in an attempt to find logical reasons for emotions. Confusion can sometimes result. They may become seriously interested in genealogy or history. This is the protector of family home or possessions.

Pallas Athena in Leo

Pallas Athena in Leo uses the technique of subtle finesse to achieve goals. A strong sense of personal security exhibits as self-confidence. These natives are closely attuned to their environment as is the good actor who responds to his audience. They know the most impressive way to approach others.

Pallas Athena in Virgo

Pallas Athena in Virgo works constructively and serves cheerfully. Creative abilities are used in practical ways. They may make a career of serving others.

Pallas Athena in Libra

Pallas Athena in Libra gives the ability to compromise with co-workers and partners to facilitate better relationships. This takes away from the executive ability, however. When one relates too closely with employees or fellow workers it is difficult to evaluate objectively. They are as aware of the rights of others as of their own.

Pallas Athena in Scorpio

Pallas Athena in Scorpio has a deep awareness of humanitarian values. Detachment in personal relationships is possible when it serves a greater purpose. By allowing outgrown ideas to be discarded, they regenerate. The placement for a good researcher, these natives discard the useless and save things of value. There is the ability to consider the overview of issues rather than mundane details.

Pallas Athena in Sagittarius

Pallas Athena in Sagittarius facilitates the ability to evaluate true personal worth enabling these natives to use their resources in the most advantageous ways. Other people may think they are lucky. Pallas wisdom is compatible with the philosophical maturity of this sign. Generally positive but not wasteful, these natives are confident and reliable. These people will use their ideas in a practical way, especially in their careers.

Pallas Athena in Capricorn

Pallas Athena in Capricorn is the position of executives who accept and carry out responsibility willingly. In evaluating the performance of a worker they consider worthwhile initiative to be as important as the final results. They judge fairly according to both ability and effort.

Pallas Athena in Aquarius

Pallas Athena in Aquarius has an excellent sense of timing which makes learning a pleasure. There is practical application of knowledge gained. These can be good astrology students. On the mental plane, they are humanitarians and like group activities.

Pallas Athena in Pisces

Pallas Athena in Pisces responds to religious experiences or ceremonies with reservation. They are concerned with the emotional impact on their free will or ego. Psychic abilities, if present, are directed to practical expressions or into daily concerns. Joy to these natives is accomplishment without having to experience the anxieties of failure. Music is the only portion of worship they allow themselves to experience. Thus, they avoid the deeper involvement which these people consider impractical.

Pallas Athena in the Houses

Pallas Athena in the First House

Pallas Athena in the first house goads these natives into being aggressive in their careers or avocations. The efficiency of Pallas is cut down in this house because there is the drive to become involved in too many projects.

Pallas Athena in the Second House

Pallas Athena in the second house has a strong desire to save and conserve. These people enjoy knowing that they have the ability to create without involving themselves in the actual physical project. Just to make the plans is often sufficient. There is enjoyment in making money as long as it does not interfere with their strict code of personal ethics. These people would never do anything which they considered wrong for gain.

Pallas Athena in the Third House

Pallas Athena in the third house gives a practical use of the mind. These people are eternally optimistic and like to talk about their work. Many of these natives teach or are in the communications field and they want people around them at all times. They seem to thrive on a variety of contacts.

Pallas Athena in the Fourth House

Pallas Athena in the fourth house creates restlessness at home. Many people with this placement work in the home, either full or part time. One native with this placement started a small purse-design business in her home. Decisions about home and family are made objectively, seeing what is best for all concerned.

Pallas Athena in the Fifth House

Pallas Athena in the fifth house combines precision

in mental exercises with self-confidence in creative activities. These people enjoy working with the public but are very sensitive to their surroundings. Inspirational and creative outlets are important for their emotional well-being. These natives enjoy chess and bridge more than golf or swim meets as a rule.

Pallas Athena in the Sixth House

Pallas Athena in the sixth house gives an interest in both raising and artistic preparation of foods. They may work in any field of service such as nursing or teaching. A careful study of the keywords will show other job trends with Pallas in this house. We do not yet know what the asteroids will mean concerning health.

Pallas Athena in the Seventh House

Pallas Athena in the seventh house determines the flow of relations. These people can usually sway others to their opinions. They are disarming because they eliminate public displays of emotion. The occupation of the partner had been shown in a few cases by the sign in which Pallas occurred in this house. In one example, Pallas in Scorpio was in the seventh house of the wife of a police detective.

Pallas Athena in the Eighth House

Pallas Athena in the eighth house is aware of humanity. Personally detached from death, it is a good placement for morticians or surgeons. There is a practical approach to handling estates or legacies. They crusade behind the scenes for causes.

Pallas Athena in the Ninth House

Pallas Athena in the ninth house gives a mature wisdom. These natives are not likely to suffer from false modesty or an inflated ego because they can assess their own worth wisely.

Pallas Athena in the Tenth House

Pallas Athena in the tenth house lightens the load of responsibility. This gives self-confidence and patience for leaders. They learn to evaluate themselves less harshly.

Pallas Athena in the Eleventh House

Pallas Athena in the eleventh house tends to handle friends and groups logically and unemotionally. Goals and ambitions are practical. There is a certain difficulty in relating closely with others. These natives are not usually found in the ranks of volunteer workers or sign-carrying zealots because they do not consider these worthwhile expenditures of energy. However, these people will certainly assist their friends in a time of actual need.

Pallas Athena in the Twelfth House

Pallas Athena in the twelfth house decreases the ability to react to spiritual ideas and experiences emotionally. These people are aware of many issues and are able to sort out what is practical and what is not. Objectivity of this type can be very helpful when serving in institutions of suffering such as hospitals.

Pallas Athena Examples

Chart 3 is an example of Pallas Athena in Cancer. For this native, the recent Saturn transit brought out a latent interest in tracing family history. He became involved in an intensive search for family records and information. From names and addresses in the family Bible he was able to contact distant relatives not only in this country but in England and Germany. Weekends were used to travel to old graveyards where relatives or ancestors were reported to be buried.

Other manifestations of this placement included the acquisition of an old house to be restored. This occurred after meeting a woman whose Venus was exactly conjunct his Pallas. With this combination of affection and business they not only married but also formed a business partnership.

To further substantiate the keywords given for Pallas Athena he plays the oboe (a wind instrument like

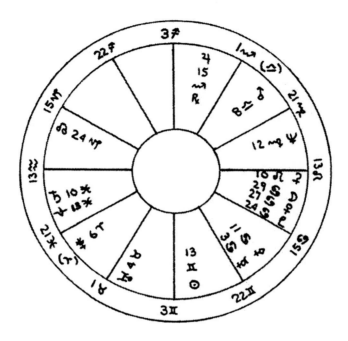

Chart 3   Male, June 4, 1935, Tropical Koch

the flute) as a hobby and has been quite active in such
conservation activities as the Audubon Society. One of
his recent creative projects was designing and hooking a
rug for his children's room.

Of course, with Mercury also present in the fifth
house it would be difficult to prove that the asteroid
Pallas makes him enjoy creative ventures that are more
mental than physical. Let us rather say that each of these
bodies enhances the effect of the other.

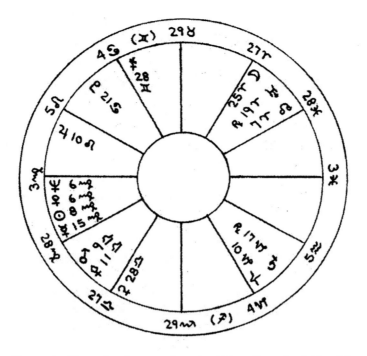

Chart 4   Female, September 1, 1931, Tropical Placidus

Another example of Pallas Athena in the chart is shown in Chart 4. With Pallas in Libra this woman executive has difficulty retaining the objectivity necessary to criticize her fellow workers. During the Uranus transit of Pallas she had an older woman as personal secretary. This secretary became progressively less efficient until she was more detriment than help. Quite practical in other fields, our native refused to complain to her superiors about this matter and would not consider firing her secretary. She excused the incompetence on grounds of ill health or family problems. The problem was solved only when the secretary retired.

Other interesting information concerning the asteroids in this chart include the fact that our native earns her living as head of a library; librarian being one of the personifications of Pallas and her Pallas is placed in the second house. Having Ceres in the third house we would expect her to talk to her cat and house plants, which she does. This native's Siamese cat is very much a part of the household. One of the most unusual facts, however, concerns the trips she plans with friends and never takes. The planning apparently satisfies her need for creativity.

With Vesta conjunct Saturn in the fifth house she cheerfully accepts the responsibility of raising her only son alone. When her marriage ended, she did not ask help, either financial or emotional, but accepted the duty quite willingly. Her parents tended the child during his early years—Vesta in the fifth house denies pleasures of raising children.

Pallas Athena, Goddess of Wisdom
Esoteric Keywords

Chakra: Heart Center/Philosophy

Colors: Indigo and lilac

Direction: East

Element: Water

Energy: Healing through magnetism

Number: 72, government through teaching
(higher vibration of 6)

Ray: Gemini, love, wisdom

Symbol: Triangle centered in a six-pointed star

Esoteric keywords for the asteroids were derived by
Dr. Elizabeth Valentine Bacon of Columbus, Ohio and
are printed with her permission.

Chapter 3

Juno

The only legal wife among the deities, Juno was the Goddess of Marriage and Maternity. According to legend, Zeus or Jupiter came to her disguised as a cuckoo. Because it was a cold winter night the young goddess warmed the chilled bird against her breast. When Jupiter assumed mortal form she demanded marriage in exchange for her favors. Thereafter, she was known as queen of the sky. Juno's fidelity to her husband was exemplary, however he was constantly unfaithful. Many interesting myths were written about Juno's attempts at revenge on her rivals and their families.

Juno was considered woman deified. In many areas temples were built to her as child-goddess, wife-goddess and widow-goddess. One of her symbols, the pomegranate, represented conjugal love and fruit-fulness. This goddess was depicted as a fully developed young woman, chaste and severe, but beautiful. Each spring she renewed her beauty by going away to bathe in special waters. When another woman boasted of having lovelier hair than Juno's the goddess turned her locks into serpents.

Just as there was no equality between Juno and Jupiter this asteroid does not represent equal relationships but the kind of legal marriages which we yet have. We must recall that women were, until recently, considered the property of father or husband. Thus, marriages were based on ability to bear heirs, housekeeping skills, virtue, family heritage, hostess abilities and feminine graces rather than any consideration of personal emotions. This was basically an employer-employee relationship where the woman was given home and security in exchange for fulfilling the duties of wife, housekeeper and mother. As with a good cow, a good wife was judged by her productiveness. The roles are occasionally reversed. For example, a man wed to a queen must agree to the number of children he will sire, as well as other responsibilities.

Juno in the chart describes how the native expects his or her mate to behave. In all cases Juno by sign described the legal mates where Venus or Mars personified the types of women or men these natives liked being around. When these planets were compatible—fine! When not, there were marital problems. For example, a man with Juno in Aries and Venus in Cancer was married to a woman with Cancer Sun. The relationship failed because he needed a more aggressive mate. In many successful marriages the male's Juno was on the female's Venus and her Juno on his Mars. One happily married couple had their respective Juno's conjunct their mates' Suns.

By legalizing relationships, Juno automatically places them into established forms and the people involved commit themselves to certain obligations and responsibilities. Then they become structured rather than free relationships. Wherever Juno is found in the horoscope it tends to restrict and structure the activities governed by that house and sign.

Juno, Goddess of Marriage

Animal: Cow

Bird: Peacock and cuckoo

Insect: Bee

Plants: Pomegranate, roses, lilies

Emblems: Linked double rings, sceptre

Principle: Legal mating

Expression: Jealousy, feminine wiles, inequality in partnerships or work, social patterns, organization in the home, fidelity, virtue, fruitful, subtlety, vindictiveness, eccentricity, grace, mating, shrewishness, birth, quarrelsome

Manifestation: Ceremonies, weddings, ornamentation, etiquette, conjugal honor, protocol, mint, cosmetics, jewelry

Personification: Bride, groom, co-ruler, co-leader, vice president, widow, hostess, housekeeper, guardian of finances, wife or husband, matron, yokemaker, eggs, sibling, heir

Juno in the Signs

Juno in Aries

Juno in Aries hopes to find strong, pioneering mates who will penalize them for all indiscretions. Either one of these partners could have literal temper tantrums to get their own way. One partner becomes the authority figure who judges the other. They like for their mates to be active in public affairs.

Juno in Taurus

Juno in Taurus personifies the iron fist in the velvet glove. With this placement comes fiscal responsibility such as needed by treasurers of large organizations or corporations. These people choose mates who are reliable and practical but have appreciation of valuable possessions.

Juno in Gemini

Juno in Gemini wants spouses who interact as playmates. Open communication is one of the benefits of these situations. For them legal alliances hamper mental freedom. They prefer structured relationships with close friends and relatives. One partner usually becomes more advanced socially or more highly educated, leaving the other behind in the position of dependent child.

Juno in Cancer

Juno in Cancer uses emotional means of getting what they feel is their due reward. This placement can mean subtle manipulation of others. When these natives feel hurt or unfairly treated they will go to any lengths to exact justice. They seek mates who are concerned with traditions and who will accept the responsibility of home and family.

Juno in Leo

Juno in Leo accentuates the drive for equality in legal partnerships. Not only do they desire perpetual lovers with a flair of showmanship but also they wish to share the spotlight with their mates. Casual affairs are difficult because of strong feelings concerning responsibility in creative relationships. They often lose their composure when faced with exceptions to their own standards.

Juno in Virgo

Juno in Virgo will be fair according to their own code of justice. They want mates who are clean almost to the point of phobia, who are precise and unassuming in public. These natives are very particular about daily details in permanent relationships. They will be fair as long as everyone is fair to them.

Juno in Libra

Juno in Libra seeks mates who are harmonious, artistic, musical and intelligent. They like beauty and balance at home. Because Libra tempers and softens energies, marital rapport may be more easily reached on mental levels than on physical planes. They believe in equal partnerships where all live up to the letter of the law.

Juno in Scorpio

Juno in Scorpio brings a strong sense of fairness and sensitivity to obligations. They like to keep things private. Strong, silent mates would appeal to these natives. This placement is difficult for open communications.

Juno in Sagittarius

Juno in Sagittarius wants freedom for both partners in relationships. They will be happy with mates who bring travel and new interests into their lives. These natives can meet and overcome their problems but they don't always. In several instances, these people were wed to their careers.

Juno in Capricorn

Juno in Capricorn brings executive ability. These people are demanding in relationships because they expect everyone to work as hard as they do. Their feelings toward others spring from their own deep sense of responsibility. Sometimes these natives serve others and are upset by lack of appreciation.

Juno in Aquarius

Juno in Aquarius restricts legal relationships. In marriage these natives do not want true equality, preferring either to adore their mates or demand subservience from them. This position structures humanitarian projects and ideas. While seeking truly free and outspoken mates they may have problems with such unusual people.

Juno in Pisces

Juno in Pisces gives the ability to subtly maneuver others into their way of thinking. This is typical of a Queen Mother working behind the scenes to lead people subconsciously into the preferred paths. Their skills vary as to the momentary need. They prefer mates who are deeply and quietly religious.

Juno in the Houses

Juno in the First House

Juno in the first house is excessively concerned with the propriety of appearances and actions. These persons consider the effect of their actions on social peer groups. Being able to organize a home makes them good hostesses and housekeepers. Mates are necessary to complete their pictures of themselves.

Juno in the Second House

Juno in the second house regiments the affections thus keeping relationships balanced so that each person gives to a certain point and then denies the partner. Even though there is polished charm neither spouse will be sympathetic to the emotional trauma of another. There is possessive intolerance of the mates' creative expressions. These natives treat their partners like library reference books—valued possessions kept on the shelves.

Juno in the Third House

Juno in the third house prefers to keep all relationships within accepted norms. Siblings and friends are supposed to fit their molds of respectability. In many ways other people hinder freedom of study and travel for these natives. Juno tends to structure the mind. There is concern with mundane social rituals.

Juno in the Fourth House

Juno in the fourth house wants traditional relationship roles observed in their homes. They will try to force their positions on their families by emotional methods. Legal spouses are important for their emotional stability. They want husbands or wives to stand by them regardless of personal feelings. One important consideration is how their mates fit into their family homes. In other words, parental approval of marriage is important.

Juno in the Fifth House

Juno in the fifth house structures creative drive or suppresses individual love nature. Creativity and purpose in others strikes a cord with these natives. Normally there is denial of any activity foreign to the established social code. They may restrict children's activities with their mates. This placement hinders love affairs.

Juno in the Sixth House

Juno in the sixth house may serve or be served by their mates. In some cases partners work together in the same offices or companies. These natives consider their marriages as accepted duties and responsibilities without much emotion. They seem married to their jobs.

Juno in the Seventh House

Juno in the seventh house brings a combination of influences. These people want everyone to fit into their patterns. Sometimes this placement brings critical females into their lives. Other people seem to control their destiny. Juno here makes people act from subconscious drives.

Juno in the Eighth House

Juno in the eighth house may attract mates with resources. There are opportunities to regenerate through their legal mates. An inner confidence makes these natives feel it unnecessary to defend their positions to others. They are adamant about carrying out their own wishes or beliefs to the extent of defying authority.

Juno in the Ninth House

Juno in the ninth house may mean that these natives travel with their partners. If these people bestow favors or gifts they expect something in return. When others do not reciprocate they are disappointed and frustrated. They have to work for benefits which they receive in life so they would not be termed lucky.

Juno in the Tenth House

Juno in the tenth house is restrictive in relationships. These people take their career responsibilities so seriously that they overextend themselves. They are very particular about their actions in public and would never openly challenge morals of the day. Mates may bring either honor or disgrace to these natives. Other people let them carry the burdens of responsibility. Sometimes these people work for their mates.

Juno in the Eleventh House

Juno in the eleventh house restricts activities with friends and groups. There can be difficulty in establishing equality and communications in legal partnerships or marriages. Just being married makes these natives feel restricted.

Juno in the Twelfth House

Juno in the twelfth house is outspoken in a proper way. Though they observe the rules of etiquette these people enjoy subtle maneuvering of others. Women with this placement use make-up skillfully. They can also be "con artists" in their fields of endeavor.

Juno Examples

Since Juno deals with ceremonies, Chart 5 is a good example to study. Here we have two wedding dates, July 3, 1954, and December 30, 1975. In each case Juno was active during that period. Transiting Juno and Venus were conjunct in 1954 and squaring the native's progressed Mars as well as trining her progressed Pallas. The transiting Sun-Uranus conjunction was semi-sextile natal Juno. On the 1975 date transiting Uranus squared natal Juno and transiting Ceres was conjunct natal Sun, transiting Juno was conjunct the South Node in the fourth house. In both cases there were trines to Ceres indicating that there would be no physical or sexual problems involved to hamper the marriage relationships. (Saturn trine Ceres in 1954 and Mercury trine Ceres in 1975.)

Two other dates of ceremonies were noted in this chart. On the day this woman was confirmed into her religion, transiting Sun and Mercury conjunct were trine her natal Juno as well as transiting Jupiter trine natal Ju-

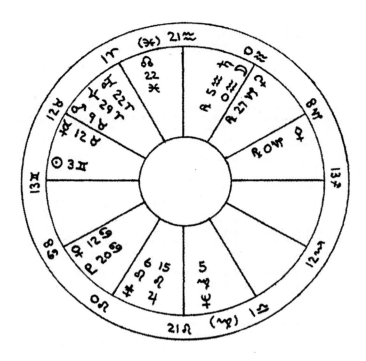

Chart 5   Female, May 24, 1932, Tropical Koch

piter. At her father's funeral in 1971 transiting Vesta
was opposite natal Juno and Pluto was trine Ceres (ruler
of the intercepted sign in her fourth house) in the eighth
house. Of course, there were other indications of the funeral.

A further example of Juno by sign and house in this
chart was her recent occupation as writer of a society
column in a local newspaper. A lot of this work involved
reporting weddings, engagements and anniversaries all

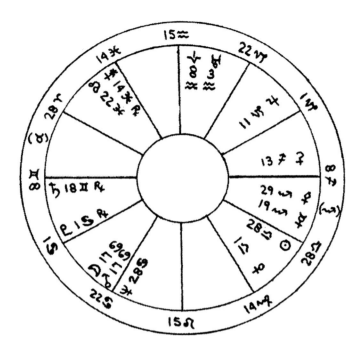

Chart 6   Female, October 21, 1913, Tropical Placidus

of which are Juno manifestations. Thus we have concern
with mundane social rituals (third house) and romantic
indications (Juno in Leo). The job was offered when
transiting Mercury, Venus and Jupiter were all trining
her natal Juno.

Juno, Goddess of Marriage
Esoteric Keywords

Chakra: Solar Plexis/Religion

Colors: Rose and blue

Direction: South

Element: Air

Energy: Social welfare or group care

Number: 108, Rosary or mala beads
(higher vibration of 9)

Ray: IV, Harmony through conflict

Symbol: Triangle in middle of a circle

Esoteric keywords for the asteroids were derived by
Dr. Elizabeth Valentine Bacon of Columbus, Ohio,
and are printed with her permission.

Chapter 4

Vesta

Vesta represents fire tamed and used for man's benefit. This Goddess of the Hearth was one of the oldest deities worshiped by man because of his respect for fire. Meals began and ended with an offering to Vesta. When members of the family left their parental homes they were given a flame of fire for their new dwellings. The fire was never allowed to go out and a very responsible member of the family was appointed to tend the fire and keep it burning. This led to the perpetual flame on the altar in places of worship.

In Egyptian and Grecian times are accounts of priestesses trained to care for the altars and tend the fires. These Vestal Virgins were dedicated to the temple between ages six and 10 where they were trained in the rituals of worship and taught the priestly traditions. The period of servitude was originally 30 years, after which they might live normal lives in the community. During this time, their primary duty was to the temple. This demonstrates delay of personal wishes until accepted responsibilities are fulfilled.

It is very important to define the slight difference between ritual and ceremony. In a religious ritual the soul is involved, whereas in ceremonies soul is not involved. Thus we would assign the service of Holy Communion to Vesta but the ceremonies of marriage and installation to Juno.

As fire was used to sterilize wounds and instruments in olden times, Vesta's association with fire shows purification. When this asteroid is aspected in the horoscope we find times of sacrifice or dedication which have a purifying effect on the native. Vesta sometimes burns out the underbrush to make way for new growth. This is taking away the debris to preserve what is important. Unlike Juno, she is not involved with daily routine matters.

Even though Vesta denies and demands sacrifices of the native these are given willingly and with a sense of dedication. This is the difference between Vesta and Saturn in astrology. Saturn imposes lessons for promotion of goals, where Vesta acts out of zealous beliefs.

When found together in the chart Vesta lightens the load for Saturn. This is like teaming two matched horses to pull the wagon; they decrease the strain on each other.

The creatures representing Vesta are all slow, steady animals who show traits of dependability and gentleness to their kind. Oak trees are noted for their longevity and ability to withstand storms. The emblem of the tripod not only represents the hearth but also is a stable, useful piece of furniture.

In representing fire that warms but never burns, Vesta in the chart shows a position where the native will deny certain personal wishes for his greater goals.

Vesta, Goddess of the Hearth

Animal: Deer, Donkey

Bird: Nightingale or ibis

Insect: Spider

Plant: Laurel or oak tree

Emblem: Tripod, flaming altar

Principle: Dedication and sacrifice

Expression: Purity, service, sacrifice, solemnity,
chastity, virginity, barrenness, purification,
preserver, security, period of servitude,
zealousness, delay, warmth, extremism

Manifestation: Ceramics, rituals, sanctuary, hearth,
fire, breaking bread together, care of ancestors,
altars, lamps, houses

Personification: Keeper of traditions, priest's
assistant, caretaker, nun or monk, acolyte,
altar guild, clubwoman or man,
Mason, Rosicrucian

Vesta in the Signs

Vesta in Aries

Vesta in Aries brings a powerful drive for perfection. These natives usually make sacrifices for causes they believe are important. They initiate work for religious and humanitarian projects. Action comes from a desire to improve every situation. There is a great deal of insecurity in self evaluation.

Vesta in Taurus

Vesta in Taurus has intense physical energies which require moral fortitude to control. There can be sacrifices of the desire nature for spiritual purposes. These natives are in constant conflict between duties and personal wishes.

Vesta in Gemini

Vesta in Gemini gives the ability to be decisive and to focus mentally on selected points. These people are willing to sacrifice for their beliefs and ideas. This placement indicates physical frigidity if the partners do not have mental rapport. Vesta here indicated either denial of offspring or sacrifices for the sake of children in the charts researched.

Vesta in Cancer

Vesta in Cancer has a strong sense of responsibility to home and family which dampens the personal emotions. Willingness to give up personal desires makes these natives appear cold and heartless at times. This conflict can create emotional disturbances when they are forced to live in unsympathetic situations. Duty to family preservation is considered a sacred trust.

Vesta in Leo

Vesta in Leo is powerful commitment versus the personal ego. In rare cases this can manifest as aesthetic or religious zealousness. These people are capable of detachment and control of private feelings. They often concentrate on their beliefs exclusively, even to the extent of refusing to consider other positions.

Vesta in Virgo

Vesta in Virgo suppresses spirit for duty. This would be like a denial of the harvest so it was not surprising to find periods of infertility with this placement. These people sacrifice their personal wishes to serve others. This is done willingly and with no regrets. At times they may nurse others through illnesses.

Vesta in Libra

Vesta in Libra denies fulfillment in relationships. These natives martyr themselves for others. They will suffer to bring about benefits for their partners. For example, one wife gave up her husband willingly when he professed a desire for a divorce. She wanted only his happiness, not thinking of herself at all.

Vesta in Scorpio

Vesta in Scorpio makes people exacting with themselves as well as with others. They seem to always be judging. This is a placement for total regeneration of the personality. It may bring psychic abilities.

Vesta in Sagittarius

Vesta in Sagittarius regulates intellectual freedom. These natives study for practical reasons rather than just pleasure of exploring new ideas. The house in which Vesta is found determines their motives for advanced training. With this placement comes extreme dedication to religious principles and strong faith.

Vesta in Capricorn

Vesta in Capricorn tends toward public martyrdom. Feeling so responsible these people will knowingly sacrifice personal fame and fortune for duty and security. Everyone is aware of their sacrifices. There are strong guilt complexes when they do not measure up to demands. These natives do not challenge authorities they consider capable.

Vesta in Aquarius

Vesta in Aquarius curbs natural freedom and aggressiveness with friends in order to carry out duties more effectively. These people realize they must deny personal hopes and desires until responsibilities are completed. Because of this control others sometimes misinterpret their emotional depths.

Vesta in Pisces

Vesta in Pisces sacrifices personality for beliefs. These may be obscure or hidden ideas which the world does not condone or understand. They dream of these ideals. Not only are these natives restrictive in relationships but also control their own actions. Feelings about others spring from hidden sources of responsibility. They undergo periods of celibacy for spiritual purposes.

Vesta in the Houses

Vesta in the First House

Vesta in the first house dreams of goals or quests. They will sacrifice family, friends, security and worldly success for those dreams. This position tests the ego. Because of this placement, these natives are critical of themselves and insecure when not following their own sets of rules. These people search for their own Holy Grail.

Vesta in the Second House

Vesta in the second house denies growth and reproduction. Depending on the aspects to this asteroid there will be variations in this manifestation. These people are strict about the use of their resources. In one case, strong aspects to Vesta denied maturity and indicated death for a child at age six.

Vesta in the Third House

Vesta in the third house makes these natives very serious and solemn in their early years. There is suppression of gaiety during elementary school ages. They are often forced to teach others regardless of their personal wishes. In every example researched, these people were mature and cautious in their communications with others. Not too outstanding in the early grades, they became good scholars as they matured.

Vesta in the Fourth House

Vesta in the fourth house accepts the duty of preserving traditional concepts of home and family. Attachment to their homes undergirds many of their actions. Sacrifices of and for the homes were found with this placement. They may have to care for invalids or older relatives in their homes.

Vesta in the Fifth House

Vesta in the fifth house denies pleasures of raising children. These people may have offspring but they are not allowed to enjoy being with them during the early years because of work situations, divorces, career dedication, family problems or other reasons. Often these are done for the security and well being of these same children. Suppression of creative urges for duties and responsibilities makes them seem cold and detached. This control of personal feelings at times expresses as personal illnesses.

Vesta in the Sixth House

Vesta in the sixth house brings restrictions and frustrations on the job. These people are willing to serve and sacrifice for their work. They know what is crucial for basic survival and how to eliminate trivia from the life. In one case, a woman with Vesta in Gemini in the sixth house teaches handcrafts and art to retarded children. She gives unlimited time and energies to this endeavor with very little thanks from her superiors. Her dedication is out of love and understanding of her pupils rather than for promotions.

Vesta in the Seventh House

Vesta in the seventh house assumes responsibility for success or failure of relationships. They give themselves for others even when the people are not closely related. There is denial of fulfillment through others.

Vesta in the Eighth House

Vesta in the eighth house denies security through the resources of partners. These natives will not receive benefits through other people for various reasons.

Vesta in the Ninth House

Vesta in the ninth house takes philosophical ideas and structures them. This placement inhibits the natural desire for travel letting a sense of duty take precedence. They will, however, travel for a purpose but not purely for enjoyment. These people take the moderate courses between extremes. Vesta here sets the mean for their groups but operates above that mean.

Vesta in the Tenth House

Vesta in the tenth house has a keen sense of responsibility and loyalty to groups and organizations. Public sacrifices are always asked of these people. They do not challenge demands made on them by higher authorities.

Vesta in the Eleventh House

Vesta in the eleventh house asks personal sacrifices for humanitarian goals. A strong conflict between need for tradition and security versus desire for freedom leaves these natives confused. They feel a threatening of their personal egos. With the perpetual swing from one extreme to another these natives force themselves to pay for their times of freedom. They feel that friends or groups should take precedence over personal ambitions.

Vesta in the Twelfth House

Vesta in the twelfth house does not bring public understanding of motives. These natives often endure deprivation for the causes in which they believe. Because these are hidden or secret beliefs other people misunderstand the reasons for their actions.

Vesta Examples

Charts showing the importance of Vesta would include multitudes who publicly dedicated their lives in various ways. Forgotten are the neighbors, friends, relatives, and clients who serve in humbler but equally important ways. Vesta shows unheralded single-minded purpose on the positive side or extremism negatively. Such a person is the example given in Chart 7.

As part of a grand trine with the Sun, Mars and Pluto in Cancer plus Pallas in Pisces, Vesta shows the great empathy with which this woman approaches others. Vesta in the sign of Scorpio makes her judgmental about her own actions, searching for understanding in every situation. Her fourth house Vesta has helped her accept the job of preserving a home and marriage despite seem-

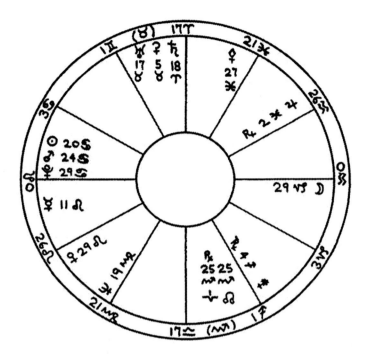

Chart 7   Female, July 13, 1938, Tropical Koch

ingly impossible difficulties. A recent attempt to divorce her alcoholic husband was delayed by his professional problems. When she approached her attorney about re-activating the suit she learned that the court had lost her file so there was no record of the divorce petition.

During this period of confusion, transiting Saturn was squaring her natal Vesta. These attempts to break up her home and throw off her marital burden were filed, dropped and then reopened during the direct, retrograde

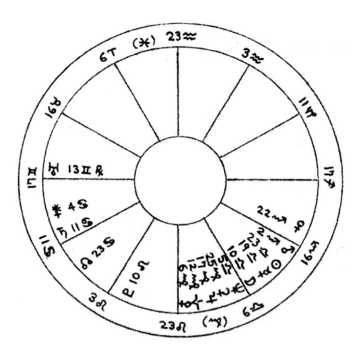

Chart 8   Female, October 15, 1944, Tropical Koch

and redirect motion of Saturn.

Rather than be discouraged with the turn of events this woman has consulted both a marriage counselor and an astrologer to discover what she has to learn from the legal relationship. She is determined to cope cheerfully and positively with her position.

Another example of Vesta is given in Chart 8. This woman had planned to open a school of metaphysics when her partner had a sudden heart attack and all plans were postponed. This happened with several planets transiting her asteroids.

In this chart Neptune was transiting in Sagittarius squaring both her Pallas and Vesta when transiting Mars squared natal Ceres, transiting Mercury squared natal Pallas and the transiting Sun squared natal Pallas. The only good aspect during this period was transiting Pluto sextile Vesta. Having three asteroids in the fourth house strengthens their effect on her home conditions. She had planned to have the school in her home (see Pallas in the fourth house) so these transits changed the plans at home as well as for the career. Her Vesta in Virgo had indicated that she would nurse someone who was seriously ill and with Ceres placed there also she will do a good job. Serving and helping other people comes naturally for her.

Another factor indicated by the placement of Vesta in Virgo was that of infertility. A few years ago she was told by her doctor that her entire endocrine system was ceasing to function. This strange malady was finally remedied but she did have a period of complete infertility.

Ceres in the fourth house makes it easy for her to cope with having large groups of people in the home. And Ceres in Virgo has the desire to nurture and care for all people with problems.

Vesta, Goddess of the Hearth
Esoteric Keywords

Chakra: Pineal Center/Higher Psychic

Colors: Ruby (pure) or lilac and amethyst

Direction: North

Element: Fire

Energy: Purification through fire

Number: 144, Government through will
(higher vibration of 12)

Ray: I, Will to good or VII, ritual

Symbol: Five pointed star

Esoteric keywords for the asteroids were derived by
Dr. Elizabeth Valentine Bacon of Columbus, Ohio,
and are printed with her permission.

Appendix A
Astronomical Data

Astrological information may be gleaned from an astronomical study of all heavenly bodies, including the little planets called asteroids. They were so named because they appear starlike when viewed through the average telescope. Their discovery was delayed because they are so faint that only Vesta can be seen with the unaided eye of man.

Table 1–Relative Brightness and Size of the Asteroids Compared with the Moon and Mercury

Object	Diameter (Km)	Relative Brightness	Discovered
Ceres (1)	1000	0.06	1801
Pallas (2)	673	0.07	1802
Juno (3)	247	0.12	1804
Vesta (4)	550	0.26	1807
Mercury	5000	0.069	—
Moon	3476	0.073	—

These relatively small particles were discovered at the beginning of the last century due to a discrepancy in Bode's Law. German scientist Johann Bode found that planets revolve around our sun in certain geometric relationships. According to his calculations, there should have been a body between the orbits of Mars and Jupiter.

An extension of this law also led to the discovery of Uranus and Neptune.

Table 2—*Positions of the Planets in the Solar System According to the Law Devised by Bode*

Planet	Distance from Sun to Earth (AU)	
	Predicted	Actual
Mercury	0.4	0.39
Venus	0.7	0.72
Earth	1.0	1.0
Mars	1.6	1.52
–	2.8	–
Jupiter	5.2	5.2
Saturn	10.0	9.5
Uranus	19.6	19.2

During the early 1800s, four of the larger asteroids—Ceres, Pallas Athena, Juno and Vesta—were sighted by leading astronomers and their positions were added in 1870 to the yearly *Nautical Almanacs*. By 1900, approximately 400 bodies had been sighted in the asteroid belt.

Certain bodies are important because of their eccentric orbits such as Hidalgo, Gounessia, Lipperta, Amor, Apollo, Adonis and Hermes.

Ephemerides of the minor planets were compiled by the Berlin Institute from 1898 to 1946. Between 1947

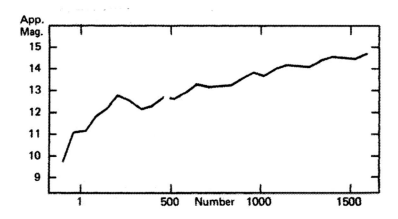

Figure 1—Asteroids were discovered according to their relative brightness as seen from Earth.

and 1951 these publications were prepared jointly by the International Minor Planet Center in Cincinnati, Ohio, and the Institute of Theoretical Astronomy in Leningrad, U.S.S.R., now published by the Russian Academy of Sciences with an English introduction and complete translation available. The Minor Planet Center recently moved from Southwestern Ohio to the Smithsonian Astrophysical Observatory in Cambridge, Massachusetts.

When Ceres or Pallas Athena are used in astronomical evaluation as representing the asteroids, per se, they fit into the anticipated patterns. Orbits of superior planets, Mars, Jupiter, Saturn, Uranus and Neptune, may be shown as multiples or echoes of each other. The 84-year period of Uranus is considered as the norm for human life expectancy, as listed in Table 3.

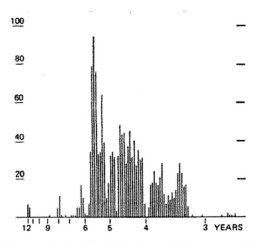

Figure 2—Orbital Cycles of the Asteroids

Table 3—Superior Planet Pattern

| Planet | Sidereal Periods | | Orbits | Life |
	Proposed	Actual		Cycle
Mars	2 years	23 months	42	1
Ceres	5 years	55 months	21	1
Jupiter	12 years	11.88 years	7	1
Saturn	30 years	29.42 years	3	1
Uranus	75 years	83.75 years	1	1
Neptune	188 years	163.74 years	½	1

However, Juno and Vesta fall short of the projected sidereal period for a planet between Mars and Jupiter according to the pattern. They have mean periods of 53 months and 41 months, respectively. All four of these asteroids remain apparently retrograde for three to four months out of each 14 to 16 months.

Table 4—Asteroid Retrograde Periods

Asteroid	Observed Number of Days Spent Retrograde		Proportion of Time Spent Retrograde
	Range	Mean	
Ceres	90-106 days	99 days	21%
Pallas	81-122 days	104 days	22%
Juno	75-115 days	101 days	22%
Vesta	86-98 days	93 days	18%

Details about this table are given in *Asteroids in the U.S.A.* Retrograde frequency for other planets may be found in *Recent Advances in Natal Astrology* by Dean and *The Book of Retrogrades* by McCormick.

In less than a decade the physical nature of asteroids has progressed from a blanket assumption that all these bodies are of the same composition to the realization that there are fundamentally different compositional groups with their own brightness and characteristics scattered about the asteroid belt. Diameters are determined by polarimetry and infrared radiometry. Some astronomers feel that most of the material reaching the earth's surface could be from the asteroids.

Current research on these and other minor solar bodies is being carried out at the Smithsonian Astrophysical Observatory in Cambridge, Massachusetts under the direction of Director Paul Herget.

References

1. Fletcher G. Watson, *Between the Planets*, Harvard University Press, 1956; *Sky and Telescope Magazine*.

2. Sagan and Leonard, *Planets*, Time-Life Books, 1968.

Suggested Reading

Ephemeris of the Asteroids Ceres, Pallas, Juno, Vesta, 1900-2000, by Bach, Celestial Communications, 1973.

An Introduction to Astronomy, by Baker, Nostrand Co., 1947.

Solar Biology, by Butler, Esoteric Fraternity Pub., 1970.

"The Nature of the Asteroids," by Chapman, *Scientific American,* January 1975, pp. 24-33.

Book of Greek Myths, by D'Aulaires, Doubleday, 1962.

Comets, Asteroids, Meteorites, edited by Delsemme, University of Toledo, 1977.

Encyclopedia of Astrology, by DeVore, Philosophical Library, 1967.

The Asteroid Ephemeris, 1883-1999, by Dobyns, Pottenger and Michelsen, TIA, 1976. *Encyclopedia Americana*

Greek Mythology, by Hamlyn, Paul Hamlyn Ltd., 1967.

70

Transpluto or Should We Call Him Bacchus Ruler of Taurus?, by Hawkins, Hawkins Enterprising Publications, 1976.

The Unknown Planets, by Jayne, Astrological Bureau, 1974.

The Gods of Egypt, by Jansky, Astro-Analytics, 1977.

Planets and Asteroids, by Leinbach, Vulcan Press, 1974.

Transits, by Leinbach, Leinbach, 1977.

Greek and Roman Mythology (4 volumes), by Lempriere, edited by Baker, SEEK, 1977.

Challenge of the Stars, by Moore and Hardy, Rand McNally, 1972.

Explanatory Supplement to the Astronomical Ephemeris and the American Ephemeris and Nautical Almanac, issued by H.M. Nautical Almanac Office, 1974.

The Asteroids, by Nourse, Watts, 1975.

Sky and Telescope Magazine, monthly columns

The Theoretic Arithmetic of the Pythagoreans, by Taylor, Weiser, 1972.

Between the Planets, by Watson, Harvard University Press, 1956.

The American Ephemeris and Nautical Almanac, U.S. Government Printing Office, yearly.

World Book Encyclopedia.

Appendix B
Positions of the Asteroids,
1900-1995

Positions of Ceres, Pallas Athena, Juno and Vesta are given for midnight Greenwich Mean Time. Ceres and Pallas have a mean sidereal period of 55 months, going retrograde every 15 to 16 months for an average of 99 and 104 days, respectively (see Table 4, Appendix A). Juno's sidereal period is 53 months, being retrograde about 101 days every 14 to 15 months. Average period for Vesta is 41 months, being retrograde for about 93 days every 16 to 17 months.

Listed positions are printed by permission of Astro-Computing Services, San Diego, California 92116.

Natal positions may be obtained by using the following tables:

Month	Days	Month	Days
January	31	July	31
February	*28	August	31
March	31	September	30
April	30	October	31
May	31	November	30
June	30	December	31

*Except leap years, when February has 29 days. A leap year occurs every fourth even-numbered year (1904, 1908, 1912, etc.). The exception is years ending in "00" unless divisible by 400. Thus, 1900 is not a leap year, but 2000 is.

1900	Jan. 1 at 0° at GMT	June 1 at 0° at GMT
Ceres	1 CP 01	15 AQ 16
Pallas	20 SA 37	26 CP 12 Rx
Juno	22 CP 21	23 PI 42
Vesta	17 AR 20	13 GE 30

1905	Jan. 1 at 0° at GMT	June 1 at 0° at GMT
Ceres	21 CP 47	13 PI 59
Pallas	9 CP 26	21 AQ 18
Juno	2 PI 31	24 TA 53
Vesta	4 LI 27	27 VI 56

1910	Jan. 1 at 0° at GMT	June 1 at 0° at GMT
Ceres	12 AQ 13	8 AR 35
Pallas	26 CP 11	10 PI 21
Juno	3 GE 03 Rx	23 CA 52
Vesta	4 AQ 22	16 AR 54

1915	Jan. 1 at 0° at GMT	June 1 at 0° at GMT
Ceres	3 PI 48	1 TA 16
Pallas	11 AQ 19	27 PI 17
Juno	23 VI 53	12 VI 16
Vesta	9 GE 42 Rx	12 CA 47

74

1920	*Jan. 1 at 0° at GMT*	*June 1 at 0° at GMT*
Ceres	27 PI 53	23 TA 47
Pallas	25 AQ 34	14 AR 54
Juno	3 SC 10	26 LI 33 Rx
Vesta	21 SC 31	00 CP 15 Rx

1925	*Jan. 1 at 0° at GMT*	*June 1 at 0° at GMT*
Ceres	27 AR 02	16 GE 34
Pallas	10 PI 36	5 TA 42
Juno	1 SA 29	13 SA 14 Rx
Vesta	12 PI 36	19 TA 15

1930	*Jan. 1 at 0° at GMT*	*June 1 at 0° at GMT*
Ceres	6 GE 25 Rx	11 CA 15
Pallas	28 PI 26	3 GE 24
Juno	28 SA 00	6 AQ 20 Rx
Vesta	15 LE 08 Rx	17 LE 06

1935	*Jan. 1 at 0° at GMT*	*June 1 at 0° at GMT*
Ceres	28 CA 35 Rx	8 LE 43
Pallas	28 AR 56	8 CA 46
Juno	28 CP 12	3 AR 44
Vesta	2 CP 10	12 PI 27

1940	*Jan. 1 at 0° at GMT*	*June 1 at 0° at GMT*
Ceres	18 VI 32	12 VI 09
Pallas	00 LE 56 Rx	15 LE 39
Juno	11 PI 43	3 GE 36
Vesta	25 AR 03	12 PI 27

1945	*Jan. 1 at 0° at GMT*	*June 1 at 0° at GMT*
Ceres	26 LI 20	24 LI 57 Rx
Pallas	5 LI 26	21 VI 24
Juno	29 GE 33 Rx	2 LE 31
Vesta	13 LI 07	9 LI 08

1950	*Jan. 1 at 0° at GMT*	*June 1 at 0° at GMT*
Ceres	24 SC 41	13 SA 25 Rx
Pallas	5 SC 53	3 SC 15 Rx
Juno	2 LI 38	20 VI 07
Vesta	10 AQ 45	22 AR 57

1955	*Jan. 1 at 0° at GMT*	*June 1 at 0° at GMT*
Ceres	17 SA 52	24 CP 56 Rx
Pallas	0 SA 15	21 SA 17 Rx
Juno	8 VI 41	4 VI 32 Rx
Vesta	20 GE 18 Rx	18 CA 15

1960	*Jan. 1 at 0° at GMT*	*June 1 at 0° at GMT*
Ceres	9 CP 19	27 AQ 47
Pallas	21 SA 33	28 CP 19 Rx
Juno	6 SA 03	22 SA 00 Rx
Vesta	28 SC 41	16 CP 42 Rx

1965	*Jan. 1 at 0° at GMT*	*June 1 at 0° at GMT*
Ceres	0 AQ 21	24 PI 34
Pallas	11 CP 07	23 AQ 27
Juno	3 CP 09	15 AQ 55
Vesta	19 PI 28	24 TA 31

1970	Jan. 1 at 0° at GMT	June 1 at 0° at GMT
Ceres	21 AQ 07	18 AR 14
Pallas	28 CP 04	12 PI 30
Juno	4 AQ 41	14 AR 04
Vesta	26 LE 07 Rx	24 LE 09

1975	Jan. 1 at 0° at GMT	June 1 at 0° at GMT
Ceres	13 PI 32	10 TA 37
Pallas	13 AQ 23	29 PI 40
Juno	22 PI 29	15 GE 28
Vesta	8 CP 45	20 PI 25

1980	Jan. 1 at 0° at GMT	June 1 at 0° at GMT
Ceres	9 AR 10	3 GE 06
Pallas	27 AQ 42	17 AR 36
Juno	25 CA 09 Rx	11 LE 10
Vesta	3 TA 27	23 GE 40

1985	Jan. 1 at 0° at GMT	June 1 at 0° at GMT
Ceres	11 TA 09	26 GE 11
Pallas	12 PI 54	9 TA 00
Juno	10 LI 24	27 VI 56
Vesta	21 LI 23	21 LI 48 SD

1990	Jan. 1 at 0° at GMT	June 1 at 0° at GMT
Ceres	25 Ge 40 Rx	21 CA 48
Pallas	1 AR 27	7 GE 40
Juno	13 SC 51	12 SC 20 Rx
Vesta	17 AQ 12	28 AR 48

1995	Jan. 1 at 0° at GMT	June 1 at 0° at GMT
Ceres	19 LE 45 Rx	21 LE 07
Pallas	5 TA 58	14 CA 00
Juno	10 SA 41	0 CP 43 Rx
Vesta	1 CA 13 Rx	23 CA 47

Appendix C
Yesterday into Tomorrow

For each question concerning the usage of asteroids in natal or personal astrology, there are hundreds when dealing with these bodies in mundane or esoteric astrology. Some writers, both ancient and contemporary, have concerned themselves with this area of space when considering time periods and cycles; others have not. Rather than delve deeply into these theories, this Appendix will merely introduce some reference materials and ideas.

In his book, *The Theory of Celestial Influence*, Rodney Collin considers the asteroid belt in the harmonic vibrations of the solar system comparing the planets to the tones of the Western musical octave as well as increasing or decreasing periods of planetary influence. He infers that the asteroids are associated with a yearly point coinciding with the date of August 27. Mr. Collins delves at length into the nine-year synodic periods of the largest mass of the asteroids. Here are correspondences with financial activity, building trades fluctuation, stock-market changes, etc., in general, economic and industrial phenomena. Because of this connection with economic conditions he further suggests that the negative influence of these cycles would be crime and corruption, recalling the legend of the fallen angel Lucifer. In the areas of human psychology and regeneration this area is positively related to perceptions (the Light of the World) and negatively to antagonists.

Upon seeing the distribution and cycle graphs of the asteroids a well known financial analyst noticed obvious trends following the ebb and flow of the stock market. This financial astrologer remarked that a huge statue of the Goddess Ceres is prominently displayed atop the famous Chicago Board of Trade Building. Hopefully, further research will be made in this area by astrologers familiar with economic trends.

The asteroids are occasionally assigned to the Eighth Scheme of Solar Evolution according to some esoteric astrologers. Arthur E. Powell discusses these phenomena in his book, *The Solar System*. He also mentions an ancient Chaldean temple arrangement whereby the asteroid belt was represented by clusters of columns topped with miniature spheres.

Earthly qualities of asteroids Vesta and Juno are briefly listed by Isabelle M. Pagan in *From Pioneer to Poet*. In his *Planets in Signs*, astrologer-author Jason Lee discusses the asteroids both in exoteric and esoteric rulership combinations.

One of the earliest and most thorough esoteric references to the asteroid belt is given in Hiram Butler's heliocentric astrology book, *Solar Biology*. He relates at length the legend of the great fragmented planet and suggests that it represented the lung area of the solar logos. The esoteric nature of the lung being to individualize or separate into positive and negative principles.

It is said that all of creation can be reduced to numerical definitions which was attempted by the disciples of Pythagoras. Part of that philosophy has been carried down through the ages as the study of Numerology. In the treatise on Pythagorean concepts, *The Theoretic Arithmetic of the Pythagoreans* by Thomas Taylor, various numerical correspondences are made with the goddesses for whom the asteroids are named. Vesta is related to the monadic number (or one) as the fire in the center of the earth which nourishes and excites from within. The feminine qualities, multiplying and duplicating, of the duad (or two) are given to Ceres along with a multitude of other deities. The pentad (or five) represents among other things justice, preventing strife, changing of qualities, and the unconquered including Pallas among its manifestations. While, under the name Minerva, this virgin goddess is connected to the Heptad (of seven) meaning motherless or ethereal. Juno, representing limitations, is listed with the deities manifesting the ennead (or nine) which forms the boundary or horizon for all the other numbers.

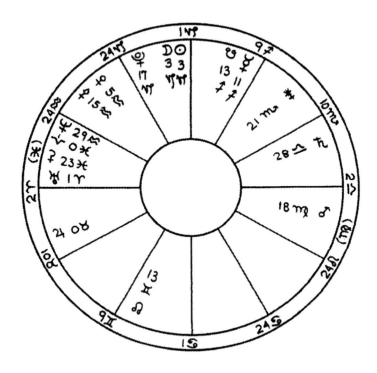

Chart 9—December 24, 2011, Tropical, Koch

For a complete understanding of the harmony of the universe this belt of asteroids must be considered, possibly along with other outer yet-undiscovered planets. Their correspondences with human chakras or glands as well as their cyclic effects upon other planets need to be researched through historical events in world cycles. It may be that the real importance of the asteroids lies in the far distant past and Earth is merely receiving the vestigial vibrations much as the human body retains formerly significant organs such as the tonsils or an appendix. If this be so then legends of the past should unlock the secrets of the future.

Frank Waters developed some interesting theories in his book, *The Mexican Mistique*, deriving data from various ancient American Indian traditions. Included was the time predicted by the Mayan calendars for the planet's entrance into a new age. That horoscope, with asteroid positions added, is given in the following chart:

References

Hiram E. Butler, *Solar Biology*, Esoteric Fraternity, 1887

Rodney Collin, *The Theory of Celestial Influence*, Samuel Weiser, 1973

Jason Lee, *Planets in Signs*, Jason Lee, England, 1978

Isabelle M. Pagan, *From Pioneer to Poet*, Theosophical Publishing House, 1930

Arthur E. Powell, *The Solar System*, Theosophical Publishing House, 1930

Thomas Taylor, *The Theoretic Arithmetic of the Pythagoreans*, Samuel Weiser, 1978

Frank Waters, *The Mexican Mistique, The Coming Sixth World of Consciousness*, The Swallow Press, Inc., 1975

Appendix D
Positions of the Asteroids, 2001-2050

Monthly positions of Ceres, Pallas Athena, Juno and Vestaare rounded off to the nearest degree from placements at midnight Greenwich Mean Time. Positions were tabulated by Wilayne Clawson of Romulus, Michigan.

Daily motion can be obtained through dividing monthly motion by days of said month. See Table 5, Appendix B.

2001

	Jan.	Feb.	Mar.	Apr.	May	June	July	Aug.	Sep.	Oct.	Nov.	Dec.
Ceres	17 SA	29 SA	9 CP	18 CP	23 CP	23 CP$_R$	18 CP$_R$	1 CP$_R$	10 CP	12 CP	20 CP	29 CP
Pallas	24 SC	5 SA	13 SA	26 SA	16 SA$_R$	8 SA$_R$	0 SA$_R$	0 SA	4 SA	13 SA	23 SA	4 CP
Juno	9 PI	24 PI	8 AR	26 AR	13 TA	2 GE	19 GE	7 CA	24 CA	9 LE	22 LE	0 VI
Vesta	26 AQ	10 PI	24 PI	8 AR	22 AR	6 TA	18 TA	0 GE	9 GE	14 GE	13 GE$_R$	7 GE$_R$

2002

	Jan.	Feb.	Mar.	Apr.	May	June	July	Aug.	Sep.	Oct.	Nov.	Dec.
Ceres	10 AQ	22 AQ	3 PI	15 PI	26 PI	6 AR	14 AR	18 AR	18 AR$_R$	12 AR$_R$	6 AR$_R$	5 AR
Pallas	16 CP	28 CP	8 AQ	18 AQ	25 AQ	0 PI	29 AQ$_R$	24 AQ$_R$	16 AQ$_R$	12 AQ$_R$	13 AQ	18 AQ
Juno	3 VI	29 LE$_R$	22 LE$_R$	18 LE$_R$	21 LE	28 LE	7 VI	18 VI	29 VI	10 LI	21 LI	2 SC
Vesta	29 TA$_R$	29 TA	4 GE	13 GE	24 GE	7 CA	20 CA	3 LE	17 LE	1 VI	15 VI	27 VI

2003

	Jan.	Feb.	Mar.	Apr.	May	June	July	Aug.	Sep.	Oct.	Nov.	Dec.
Ceres	8 AR	17 AR	26 AR	8 TA	20 TA	2 GE	15 GE	27 GE	8 CA	18 CA	25 CA	27 CA$_R$
Pallas	26 AQ	5 PI	14 PI	25 PI	5 AR	14 AR	22 AR	28 AR	29 AR$_R$	25 AR$_R$	16 AR$_R$	10 AR$_R$
Juno	11 SC	18 SC	21 SC	20 SC$_R$	14 SC$_R$	8 SC$_R$	6 SC	8 SC	14 SC	22 SC	2 SA	12 SA
Vesta	6 LI	13 LI	13 LI$_R$	8 LI$_R$	2 LI$_R$	2 LI	8 LI	18 LI	2 SC	17 SC	3 SA	20 SA

2004

	Jan.	Feb.	Mar.	Apr.	May	June	July	Aug.	Sep.	Oct.	Nov.	Dec.
Ceres	22 CA$_R$	15 CA$_R$	13 CA	17 CA	25 CA	6 LE	18 LE	2 VI	16 VI	0 LI	14 LI	27 LI
Pallas	13 AR	21 AR	3 TA	18 TA	4 GE	23 GE	11 CA	29 CA	17 LE	3 VI	18 VI	1 LI
Juno	23 SA	4 CP	13 CP	21 CP	25 CP	26 CP$_R$	21 CP$_R$	14 CP$_R$	11 CP	13 CP	20 CP	0 AQ
Vesta	6 CP	23 CP	8 AQ	23 AQ	7 PI	19 PI	27 PI	1 AR	27 PI$_R$	20 PI$_R$	16 PI$_R$	19 PI

2005

	Jan.	Feb.	Mar.	Apr.	May	June	July	Aug.	Sep.	Oct.	Nov.	Dec.
Ceres	9 SC	19 SC	25 SC	26 SC$_R$	21 SC$_R$	15 SC$_R$	13 SC	16 SC	23 SC	3 SA	14 SA	26 SA
Pallas	11 LI	15 LI	13 LI$_R$	4 LI$_R$	27 VI$_R$	27 VI	3 LI	13 LI	24 L	6 SC	20 SC	3 SA
Juno	13 AQ	27 AQ	10 PI	26 PI	11 AR	27 AR	13 TA	28 TA	12 GE	3 GE	29 GE	27 GE$_R$
Vesta	27 PI	8 AR	19 AR	2 TA	15 TA	29 TA	12 GE	25 GE	5 CA	14 CA	20 CA	21 CA$_R$

	Jan.	Feb.	Mar.	Apr.	May	June	July	Aug.	Sep.	Oct.	Nov.	Dec.
2006												
Ceres	9 CP	21 CP	2 AQ	12 AQ	21 AQ	26 AQ	27 AQ_R	23 AQ_R	16 AQ_R	13 AQ_R	16 AQ	22 AQ
Pallas	15 SA	29 SA	9 CP	17 CP	21 CP	20 CP_R	13 CP_R	5 CP_R	3 CP	6 CP	12 CP	21 CP
Juno	19 GE_R	18 GE	23 GE	3 CA	16 CA	0 LE	13 LE	27 LE	10 VI	23 VI	5 LI	15 LI
Vesta	16 CA_R	9 CA_R	7 CA	10 CA	18 CA	0 LE	13 LE	28 LE	12 VI	27 VI	13 LI	28 LI
2007												
Ceres	1 PI	12 PI	23 PI	5 AR	17 AR	29 AR	9 TA	18 TA	23 TA	24 TA_R	20 TA_R	13 TA_R
Pallas	3 AQ	12 AQ	23 AQ	3 PI	11 PI	17 PI	20 PI	19 PI_R	12 PI_R	5 PI_R	2 PI	4 PI
Juno	23 LI	28 LI	28 LI_R	23 LI_R	16 LI_R	13 LI_R	15 LI	20 LI	28 LI	7 SC	18 SC	28 SC
Vesta	13 SC	26 SC	7 SA	16 SA_R	18 SA_R	13 SA_R	7 SA_R	6 SA	12 SA	22 SA	4 CP	20 CP
2008												
Ceres	10 TA	14 TA	21 TA	1 GE	13 GE	26 GE	9 CA	22 CA	6 LE	18 LE	0 VI	9 VI
Pallas	11 PI	20 PI	0 AR	11 AR	23 AR	6 TA	18 TA	0 GE	11 GE	20 GE	24 GE_R	18 GE_R
Juno	8 SA	18 SA	25 SA	0 CP	0 CP_R	26 SA_R	19 SA_R	15 SA_R	16 SA	22 SA	0 CP	11 CP
Vesta	6 AQ	21 AQ	6 PI	21 PI	5 AR	19 AR	0 TA	10 TA	16 TA	15 TA_R	7 TA_R	1 TA_R
2009												
Ceres	14 VI	13 VI_R	8 VI_R	2 VI_R	2 VI	8 VI	18 VI	29 VI	12 LI	25 LI	9 SC	22 SC
Pallas	7 GE_R	9 GE	16 GE	0 CA	14 CA	0 LE	15 LE	1 VI	16 VI	0 LI	15 LI	28 LI
Juno	22 CP	4 AQ	17 AQ	0 PI	12 PI	23 PI	3 AR	8 AR	8 AR_R	2 AR_R	27 PI_R	29 PI
Vesta	0 TA	15 TA	13 TA	24 TA	6 GE	19 GE	2 CA	16 CA	29 CA	11 LE	23 LE	1 VI
2010												
Ceres	5 SA	17 SA	26 SA	3 CP	5 CP_R	2 CP_R	26 SA_R	21 SA_R	23 SA	28 SA	7 CP	17 CP
Pallas	10 SC	19 SC	25 SC	25 SC_R	18 SC_R	10 SC_R	7 SC	11 SC	19 SC	29 SC	11 SA	23 SA
Juno	8 AR	22 AR	6 TA	24 TA	11 GE	28 GE	15 CA	1 LE	17 LE	1 VI	14 VI	24 VI
Vesta	6 VI	4 VI_R	27 LE_R	21 LE_R	22 LE	29 LE	10 VI	23 VI	8 LI	21 LI	8 SC	26 SC

	Jan.	Feb.	Mar.	Apr.	May	June	July	Aug.	Sep.	Oct.	Nov.	Dec.
2011												
Ceres	29 CP	11 AQ	22 AQ	4 PI	14 PI	23 PI	29 PI	0 AR$_R$	27 PI$_R$	21 PI$_R$	17 PI$_R$	18 PI
Pallas	6 CP	18 CP	28 CP	8 AQ	15 AQ	18 AQ	15 AQ	8 AQ$_R$	1 AQ$_R$	29 CP	2 AQ	9 AQ
Juno	1 LI	2 LI$_R$	27 VI$_R$	20 VI$_R$	16 VI$_R$	18 VI	24 VI	2 LI	12 LI	22 LI	3 SC	13 SC
Vesta	13 SA	0 CP	14 CP	28 CP	10 AQ	19 AQ	21 AQ$_R$	17 AQ$_R$	10 AQ$_R$	8 AQ	13 AQ	21 AQ
2012												
Ceres	25 PI	4 AR	15 AR	27 AR	9 TA	21 TA	3 GE	14 GE	24 GE	1 CA	4 CA	1 CA$_R$
Pallas	17 AQ	27 AQ	7 PI	17 PI	26 PI	5 AR	20 AR	13 AR	10 AR$_R$	3 AR$_R$	26 PI$_R$	24 PI
Juno	23 SC	1 SA	7 SA	8 SA$_R$	5 SA$_R$	28 SC$_R$	23 SC$_R$	23 SC	27 SC	4 SA	14 SA	24 SA
Vesta	3 PI	17 PI	0 AR	12 AR	28 AR	12 TA	24 TA	6 GE	16 GE	23 GE	24 GE$_R$	21 GE$_R$
2013												
Ceres	24 GE$_R$	20 GE$_R$	22 GE	29 GE	9 CA	21 CA	4 LE	18 LE	2 VI	16 VI	29 VI	12 LI
Pallas	29 PI	8 AR	18 AR	2 TA	17 TA	3 GE	20 GE	8 CA	26 CA	13 LE	28 LE	10 VI
Juno	6 CP	17 CP	27 CP	7 AQ	15 AQ	21 AQ	21 AQ$_R$	16 AQ$_R$	9 AQ$_R$	7 AQ	11 AQ	20 AQ
Vesta	13 GE$_R$	1 GE	12 GE	20 GE	0 CA	12 CA	25 CA	9 LE	24 LE	8 VI	22 VI	5 LI
2014												
Ceres	23 LI	1 SC	3 SC$_R$	29 LI$_R$	23 LI$_R$	20 LI$_R$	22 LI	29 LI	9 SC	20 SC	2 SA	15 SA
Pallas	17 VI	15 VI$_R$	6 VI$_R$	29 LE$_R$	29 LE	6 VI	16 VI	28 VI	11 LI	24 LI	7 SC	20 SC
Juno	2 PI	17 PI	2 AR	19 AR	6 TA	24 TA	12 GE	29 GE	16 CA	1 LE	13 LE	21 LE
Vesta	22 LI	28 LI	3 SC	1 SC$_R$	24 LI$_R$	20 LI$_R$	23 LI	1 SC	14 SC	27 SC	13 SA	28 SA
2015												
Ceres	28 SA	10 CP	20 CP	0 AQ	7 AQ	10 AQ	8 AQ$_R$	2 AQ$_R$	26 CP$_R$	26 CP	2 AQ	10 AQ
Pallas	4 SA	16 SA	25 SA	2 CP	3 CP$_R$	28 SA$_R$	19 SA$_R$	15 SA$_R$	16 SA	23 SA	2 CP	12 CP
Juno	21 LE$_R$	15 LE$_R$	9 LE$_R$	8 LE	13 LE	22 LE	2 VI	13 VI	25 LI	7 LI	18 LI	28 LI
Vesta	15 CP	1 AQ	16 AQ	1 PI	14 PI	27 PI	7 AR	13 AR	13 AR$_R$	8 AR$_R$	1 AR$_R$	0 AR

	Jan.	Feb.	Mar.	Apr.	May	June	July	Aug.	Sep.	Oct.	Nov.	Dec.
2016												
Ceres	20 AQ	2 PI	13 PI	25 PI	6 AR	17 AR	26 AR	3 TA	6 TA	3 TA$_R$	26 AR$_R$	22 AR$_R$
Pallas	23 CP	5 AQ	15 AQ	25 AQ	2 PI	8 PI	8 PI$_R$	5 PI$_R$	27 AQ$_R$	22 AQ$_R$	21 AQ	25 AQ
Juno	7 SC	14 SC	17 SC	14 SC$_R$	8 SC$_R$	2 SC$_R$	0 SC	4 SC	11 SC	19 SC	29 SC	9 SA
Vesta	6 AR	15 AR	26 AR	9 TA	21 TA	5 GE	17 GE	0 CA	13 CA	23 CA	2 LE	6 LE
2017												
Ceres	22 AR	29 AR	8 TA	19 TA	1 GE	14 GE	26 GE	9 CA	22 CA	3 LE	12 LE	18 LE
Pallas	2 PI	12 PI	21 PI	2 AR	12 AR	23 AR	3 TA	11 TA	16 TA	16 TA$_R$	8 TA$_R$	29 AR$_R$
Juno	20 SA	0 CP	9 CP	16 CP	20 CP	19 CP$_R$	14 CP$_R$	7 CP$_R$	5 CP	8 CP	16 CP	26 CP
Vesta	3 LE$_R$	25 CA$_R$	21 CA$_R$	21 CA	28 CA	9 LE	21 LE	5 VI	20 VI	5 LI	21 LI	6 SC
2018												
Ceres	18 LE$_R$	13 LE$_R$	7 LE$_R$	6 LE	11 LE	21 LE	2 VI	15 VI	28 VI	12 LI	26 LI	9 SC
Pallas	28 AR	6 TA	17 TA	3 GE	20 GE	8 CA	26 CA	14 LE	0 VI	16 VI	0 LI	13 LI
Juno	8 AQ	22 AQ	5 PI	20 PI	4 AR	19 AR	4 TA	18 TA	0 GE	8 GE	9 GE$_R$	3 GE$_R$
Vesta	22 SC	7 SA	20 SA	1 CP	8 CP	8 CP$_R$	2 CP$_R$	26 SA$_R$	27 SA	5 CP	16 CP	29 CP
2019												
Ceres	22 SC	3 SA	11 SA	15 SA	14 SA$_R$	8 SA$_R$	3 SA$_R$	2 SA	7 SA	16 SA	25 SA	6 CP
Pallas	24 LI	2 SC	3 SC$_R$	28 LI$_R$	19 LI$_R$	14 LI$_R$	16 LI	25 LI	4 SC	16 SC	29 SC	12 SA
Juno	29 TA$_R$	3 GE	12 GE	25 GE	9 CA	23 CA	7 LE	22 LE	6 VI	17 VI	0 LI	11 LI
Vesta	13 AQ	28 AQ	12 PI	27 PI	11 AR	25 AR	7 TA	18 TA	25 TA	27 TA$_R$	24 TA$_R$	17 TA$_R$
2020												
Ceres	19 CP	1 AQ	12 AQ	23 AQ	3 PI	10 PI	13 PI	12 PI$_R$	6 PI$_R$	0 PI$_R$	29 AQ	4 PI
Pallas	25 SA	7 CP	18 CP	27 CP	3 AQ	3 AQ$_R$	28 CP$_R$	20 CP$_R$	15 CP$_R$	16 CP	22 CP	0 AQ
Juno	17 LI	22 LI	21 LI$_R$	16 LI$_R$	10 LI$_R$	8 LI$_R$	10 LI	16 LI	25 LI	4 SC	15 SC	25 SC
Vesta	12 TA	15 TA	22 TA	2 GE	13 GE	27 GE	10 CA	23 CA	7 LE	20 LE	2 VI	13 VI

2021	Jan.	Feb.	Mar.	Apr.	May	June	July	Aug.	Sep.	Oct.	Nov.	Dec.
Ceres	12 PI	23 PI	3 AR	16 AR	28 AR	10 TA	21 TA	1 GE	9 GE	13 GE	12 GE$_R$	5 GE$_R$
Pallas	9 AQ	20 AQ	29 AQ	9 PI	17 PI	25 PI	29 PI	29 PI$_R$	24 PI$_R$	16 PI$_R$	11 PI	12 PI
Juno	5 SA	14 SA	21 SA	25 SA	25 SA$_R$	20 SA$_R$	13 SA$_R$	10 SA	12 SA	18 SA	27 SA	7 CP
Vesta	21 VI	21 VI$_R$	18 VI$_R$	10 VI$_R$	7 VI	12 VI	21 VI	4 LI	18 LI	3 SC	20 SC	6 SA

2022	Jan.	Feb.	Mar.	Apr.	May	June	July	Aug.	Sep.	Oct.	Nov.	Dec.
Ceres	29 TA$_R$	29 TA	5 GE	14 GE	25 GE	8 CA	21 CA	4 LE	18 LE	2 VI	14 VI	26 VI
Pallas	18 PI	27 PI	7 AR	19 AR	2 TA	16 TA	0 GE	16 GE	1 CA	15 CA	28 CA	4 LE$_R$
Juno	19 CP	1 AQ	12 AQ	25 AQ	6 PI	16 PI	23 PI	26 PI$_R$	23 PI$_R$	16 PI$_R$	13 PI	18 PI
Vesta	23 SA	9 CP	23 CP	9 AQ	21 AQ	2 PI	8 PI	8 PI$_R$	1 PI$_R$	25 AQ$_R$	25 AQ$_R$	2 PI

2023	Jan.	Feb.	Mar.	Apr.	May	June	July	Aug.	Sep.	Oct.	Nov.	Dec.
Ceres	4 LI	8 LI	6 LI$_R$	29 VI$_R$	25 VI$_R$	27 VI	4 LI	13 LI	25 LI	7 SC	20 SC	3 SA
Pallas	0 LE$_R$	21 CA$_R$	18 CA$_R$	23 CA	3 LE	16 LE	29 LE	13 VI	27 VI	10 LI	24 LI	8 SC
Juno	28 PI	13 AR	28 AR	15 TA	3 GE	21 GE	8 CA	25 CA	11 LE	25 LE	8 VI	18 VI
Vesta	12 PI	23 PI	7 AR	21 AR	4 TA	18 TA	1 GE	13 GE	23 GE	2 CA	7 CA	5 CA$_R$

2024	Jan.	Feb.	Mar.	Apr.	May	June	July	Aug.	Sep.	Oct.	Nov.	Dec.
Ceres	16 SA	28 SA	8 CP	17 CP	22 CP	21 CP$_R$	16 CP$_R$	10 CP$_R$	8 CP	12 CP	19 CP	28 CP
Pallas	20 SC	1 SA	9 SA	13 SA	9 SA$_R$	0 SA$_R$	24 SC$_R$	24 SC	1 SA	10 SA	20 SA	2 CP
Juno	24 VI	24 VI$_R$	18 VI$_R$	11 VI$_R$	9 VI	13 VI	20 VI	29 VI	9 LI	19 LI	0 SC	11 SC
Vesta	28 GE$_R$	22 GE$_R$	22 GE	28 GE	7 CA	19 CA	2 LE	16 LE	1 VI	15 VI	0 LI	15 LI

2025	Jan.	Feb.	Mar.	Apr.	May	June	July	Aug.	Sep.	Oct.	Nov.	Dec.
Ceres	9 AQ	21 AQ	2 PI	14 PI	25 PI	5 AR	13 AR	17 AR	15 AR$_R$	11 AR$_R$	5 AR$_R$	3 AR
Pallas	14 CP	26 CP	6 AQ	16 AQ	23 AQ	27 AQ	26 AQ$_R$	20 SC$_R$	12 AQ$_R$	9 AQ$_R$	10 AQ	16 AQ
Juno	20 SC	28 SC	2 SA	3 SA$_R$	29 SC$_R$	22 SC$_R$	18 SC$_R$	18 SC	24 SC	1 SA	11 SA	21 SA
Vesta	28 LI	10 SC	18 SC	21 SC$_R$	18 SC$_R$	11 SC	9 SC	14 SC	24 SC	7 SA	21 SA	7 CP

2026

	Jan.	Feb.	Mar.	Apr.	May	June	July	Aug.	Sep.	Oct.	Nov.	Dec.
Ceres	8 AR	16 AR	25 AR	7 TA	19 TA	2 GE	14 GE	26 GE	8 CA	17 CA	23 CA	24 CA$_R$
Pallas	24 AQ	4 PI	13 PI	23 PI	28 PI	12 AR	20 AR	24 AR	24 AR$_R$	19 AR$_R$	10 AR$_R$	6 AR
Juno	2 CP	13 CP	23 CP	2 AQ	10 AQ	14 AQ	12 AQ$_R$	6 AQ$_R$	29 CP$_R$	29 CP	4 AQ	14 AQ
Vesta	22 CP	8 AQ	22 AQ	7 PI	26 PI	5 AR	16 AR	24 AR	28 AR	24 AR$_R$	16 AR$_R$	12 AR$_R$

2027

	Jan.	Feb.	Mar.	Apr.	May	June	July	Aug.	Sep.	Oct.	Nov.	Dec.
Ceres	20 CA$_R$	13 CA$_R$	11 CA	15 CA	23 CA	5 LE	17 LE	1 VI	15 VI	28 VI	13 LI	26 LI
Pallas	9 AR	17 AR	28 AR	13 TA	29 TA	17 GE	5 CA	24 CA	12 LE	28 LE	14 VI	26 VI
Juno	26 AQ	11 PI	25 PI	12 AR	28 AR	16 TA	3 GE	21 GE	7 CA	22 CA	4 LE	10 LE
Vesta	14 AR	22 AR	1 TA	13 TA	26 TA	9 GE	22 GE	5 CA	18 CA	0 LE	10 LE	16 LE

2028

	Jan.	Feb.	Mar.	Apr.	May	June	July	Aug.	Sep.	Oct.	Nov.	Dec.
Ceres	8 SC	18 SC	23 SC	23 SC$_R$	19 SC$_R$	13 SC$_R$	11 SC	15 SC	22 SC	2 SA	14 SA	26 SA
Pallas	6 LI	9 LI	5 LI$_R$	25 VI$_R$	19 VI$_R$	21 VI	29 VI	9 LI	21 LI	3 SC	17 SC	0 SA
Juno	8 LE$_R$	0 LE$_R$	26 CA$_R$	28 CA	6 LE	16 LE	27 LE	9 VI	21 VI	3 LI	15 LI	25 LI
Vesta	17 LE$_R$	12 LE$_R$	5 LE$_R$	2 LE	7 LE	16 LE	28 LE	12 VI	27 VI	12 LI	28 LI	14 SC

2029

	Jan.	Feb.	Mar.	Apr.	May	June	July	Aug.	Sep.	Oct.	Nov.	Dec.
Ceres	8 CP	20 CP	1 AQ	12 AQ	20 AQ	25 AQ	26 AQ$_R$	21 AQ$_R$	15 AQ$_R$	12 AQ$_R$	14 AQ	21 AQ
Pallas	13 SA	26 SA	6 CP	14 CP	17 CP	14 CP$_R$	7 CP$_R$	0 SC	28 SA	3 CP	11 CP	20 CP
Juno	4 SC	10 SC	12 SC	9 SC$_R$	2 SC$_R$	27 LI$_R$	26 LI	0 SC	7 SC	15 SC	26 SC	6 SA
Vesta	1 SA	17 SA	0 CP	13 CP	22 CP	27 CP	24 CP	18 CP$_R$	14 CP$_R$	17 CP	26 CP	7 AQ

2030

	Jan.	Feb.	Mar.	Apr.	May	June	July	Aug.	Sep.	Oct.	Nov.	Dec.
Ceres	1 PI	12 PI	23 PI	5 AR	17 AR	28 AR	8 TA	17 TA	22 TA	22 TA$_R$	18 TA$_R$	11 TA$_R$
Pallas	1 AQ	11 AQ	21 AQ	1 PI	9 PI	15 PI	18 PI	15 PI$_R$	8 PI$_R$	1 PI$_R$	29 AQ	2 PI
Juno	17 SA	27 SA	5 CP	11 CP	14 CP	12 CP$_R$	6 CP$_R$	0 CP$_R$	29 SA	3 CP	11 CP	21 CP
Vesta	21 AQ	5 PI	19 PI	3 AR	17 AR	1 TA	13 TA	25 TA	4 GE	8 GE	7 GE$_R$	1 GE$_R$

	Jan.	Feb.	Mar.	Apr.	May	June	July	Aug.	Sep.	Oct.	Nov.	Dec.
2031												
Ceres	9 TA	13 TA	20 TA	0 GE	12 GE	25 GE	8 CA	21 CA	5 LE	17 LE	28 LE	7 VI
Pallas	9 PI	18 PI	27 PI	9 AR	20 AR	2 TA	14 TA	25 TA	5 GE	20 GE	11 GE_R	3 GE_R
Juno	3 AQ	17 AQ	29 AQ	14 PI	28 PI	12 AR	25 AR	7 TA	16 TA	20 TA_R	16 TA_R	10 TA_R
Vesta	23 TA_R	22 TA	28 TA	7 GE	18 GE	1 CA	14 CA	28 CA	11 LE	25 LE	8 VI	20 VI
2032												
Ceres	12 VI	11 VI_R	5 VI_R	0 VI_R	0 VI	7 VI	16 VI	29 VI	11 LI	25 LI	8 SC	21 SC
Pallas	25 TA_R	27 TA	8 GE	22 GE	8 CA	25 CA	11 LE	27 LE	12 VI	27 VI	11 LI	24 LI
Juno	11 TA	19 TA	1 GE	16 GE	1 CA	17 CA	2 LE	17 LE	1 VI	14 VI	26 VI	7 LI
Vesta	1 LI	7 LI	6 LI_R	0 LI_R	24 VI_R	25 VI	2 LI	13 LI	27 LI	12 SC	28 SC	14 SA
2033												
Ceres	4 SA	16 SA	25 SA	2 CP	4 CP_R	0 CP_R	24 SA_R	20 SA_R	21 SA	28 SA	7 CP	17 CP
Pallas	6 SC	15 SC	20 SC	19 SC_R	11 SC_R	3 SC_R	2 SC	7 SC	16 SC	26 SC	8 SA	21 SA
Juno	14 LI	18 LI	16 LI_R	9 LI_R	3 LI_R	2 LI	6 LI	13 LI	21 LI	1 SC	12 SC	22 SC
Vesta	0 CP	17 CP	2 AQ	17 AQ	0 PI	12 PI	20 PI	24 PI	20 PI_R	13 PI_R	9 PI_R	12 PI
2034												
Ceres	29 CP	11 AQ	22 AQ	3 PI	14 PI	23 PI	28 PI	29 PI_R	25 PI_R	19 PI_R	15 PI_R	17 PI
Pallas	4 CP	16 CP	26 CP	6 AQ	12 AQ	14 AQ	10 AQ_R	2 AQ_R	26 CP_R	25 CP	28 CP	6 AQ
Juno	2 SA	11 SA	17 SA	20 SA	19 SA_R	13 SA_R	7 SA_R	4 SA	8 SA	14 SA	23 SA	3 CP
Vesta	21 PI	2 AR	13 AR	26 AR	10 TA	23 TA	6 GE	19 GE	0 CA	10 CA	16 CA	17 CA_R
2035												
Ceres	24 PI	4 AR	14 AR	26 AR	8 TA	20 TA	2 GE	13 GE	23 GE	0 CA	2 CA_R	29 GE_R
Pallas	15 AQ	26 AQ	5 PI	15 PI	24 PI	2 AR	8 AR	10 AR	6 AR_R	28 PI_R	21 PI_R	21 PI
Juno	14 CP	26 CP	7 AQ	19 AQ	28 AQ	8 PI	14 PI	14 PI_R	8 PI_R	2 PI_R	1 PI	8 PI
Vesta	12 CA_R	4 CA_R	2 CA	6 CA	14 CA	25 CA	8 LE	22 LE	7 VI	21 VI	7 LI	22 LI

2036

	Jan.	Feb.	Mar.	Apr.	May	June	July	Aug.	Sep.	Oct.	Nov.	Dec.
Ceres	23 GE$_R$	19 GE$_R$	20 GE	28 GE	8 CA	21 CA	3 LE	17 LE	1 VI	15 VI	29 VI	11 LI
Pallas	26 PI	5 AR	15 AR	29 AR	13 TA	29 TA	15 GE	2 CA	20 CA	7 LE	22 LE	3 VI
Juno	20 PI	4 AR	20 AR	8 TA	25 TA	14 GE	1 CA	18 CA	5 LE	19 LE	2 VI	12 VI
Vesta	7 SC	21 SC	2 SA	10 SA	11 SA$_R$	5 SA$_R$	29 SC$_R$	29 SC	6 SA	17 CP	0 CP	15 CP

2037

	Jan.	Feb.	Mar.	Apr.	May	June	July	Aug.	Sep.	Oct.	Nov.	Dec.
Ceres	22 LI	29 LI	1 VI$_R$	28 LI$_R$	21 LI$_R$	18 LI$_R$	21 LI	28 LI	8 SC	19 SC	2 SA	14 SA
Pallas	8 VI	3 VI$_R$	25 LE$_R$	20 LE	23 LE	1 VI	12 VI	24 VI	7 LI	21 LI	4 SC	18 SC
Juno	17 VI	14 VI$_R$	8 VI$_R$	2 VI$_R$	2 VI	7 VI	15 VI	24 VI	5 LI	16 LI	27 LI	7 SC
Vesta	0 AQ	16 AQ	0 PI	15 PI	29 PI	13 AR	24 AR	4 TA	9 TA	9 TA$_R$	2 TA$_R$	26 AR$_R$

2038

	Jan.	Feb.	Mar.	Apr.	May	June	July	Aug.	Sep.	Oct.	Nov.	Dec.
Ceres	27 SA	9 CP	20 CP	29 CP	6 AQ	9 AQ	6 AQ$_R$	0 AQ$_R$	25 CP$_R$	25 CP	1 AQ	9 AQ
Pallas	1 SA	12 SA	21 SA	28 SA	28 SA$_R$	21 SA$_R$	13 SA$_R$	9 SA$_R$	12 SA	20 SA	29 SA	10 CP
Juno	17 SC	24 SC	28 SC	28 SC$_R$	23 SC$_R$	17 SC$_R$	13 SC$_R$	14 SC	20 SC	28 SC	7 SA	18 SA
Vesta	25 AR	1 TA	9 TA	20 TA	2 GE	15 GE	28 GE	12 CA	25 CA	7 LE	19 LE	27 LE

2039

	Jan.	Feb.	Mar.	Apr.	May	June	July	Aug.	Sep.	Oct.	Nov.	Dec.
Ceres	19 AQ	1 PI	12 PI	24 PI	6 AR	16 AR	25 AR	2 TA	5 TA	1 TA$_R$	24 AR$_R$	20 AR$_R$
Pallas	21 CP	3 AQ	13 AQ	22 AQ	0 PI	5 PI	6 PI$_R$	1 PI$_R$	24 AQ$_R$	19 AQ$_R$	18 AQ	23 AQ
Juno	29 SA	10 CP	19 CP	29 CP	4 AQ	7 AQ$_R$	4 AQ$_R$	27 CP$_R$	21 CP$_R$	22 CP	28 CP	8 AQ
Vesta	2 VI	29 LE$_R$	22 LE$_R$	17 LE$_R$	18 LE	26 LE	7 VI	20 VI	5 LI	20 LI	7 SC	23 SC

2040

	Jan.	Feb.	Mar.	Apr.	May	June	July	Aug.	Sep.	Oct.	Nov.	Dec.
Ceres	21 AR	28 AR	7 TA	18 TA	0 GE	13 GE	26 GE	9 CA	21 CA	2 LE	11 LE	17 LE
Pallas	0 PI	9 PI	19 PI	0 AR	10 AR	20 AR	29 AR	7 TA	11 TA	8 TA$_R$	29 AR$_R$	22 AR$_R$
Juno	21 AQ	5 PI	19 PI	5 AR	22 AR	9 TA	26 TA	12 GE	28 GE	12 CA	22 CA	25 CA$_R$
Vesta	9 SA	26 SA	10 CP	24 CP	6 AQ	14 AQ	16 AQ$_R$	11 AQ$_R$	4 AQ$_R$	2 AQ	8 AQ	17 AQ

2041

	Jan.	Feb.	Mar.	Apr.	May	June	July	Aug.	Sep.	Oct.	Nov.	Dec.
Ceres	16 LE$_R$	10 LE$_R$	5 LE$_R$	5 LE	10 LE	20 LE	1 VI	14 VI	5 LI	11 LI	25 LI	9 SC
Pallas	23 AR	1 TA	12 TA	28 TA	15 GE	3 CA	21 CA	9 LE	26 LE	12 VI	27 VI	10 LI
Juno	20 CA$_R$	14 CA$_R$	13 CA	19 CA	28 CA	10 LE	22 LE	5 VI	17 VI	29 VI	11 LI	21 LI
Vesta	0 PI	13 PI	26 PI	10 AR	24 AR	8 TA	20 TA	2 GE	12 GE	19 GE	20 GE$_R$	15 GE$_R$

2042

	Jan.	Feb.	Mar.	Apr.	May	June	July	Aug.	Sep.	Oct.	Nov.	Dec.
Ceres	21 SC	2 SA	10 SA	14 SA	12 SA$_R$	6 SA$_R$	1 SA$_R$	1 SA	6 SA	14 SA	25 SA	6 CP
Pallas	20 LI	26 LI	26 LI$_R$	20 LI	11 LI$_R$	8 LI	12 LI	20 LI	1 SC	13 SC	26 SC	9 SA
Juno	0 SC	6 SC	6 SC$_R$	2 SC$_R$	26 LI$_R$	21 LI$_R$	12 LI	26 LI	4 SC	13 SC	23 SC	3 SA
Vesta	8 GE$_R$	4 GE	8 GE	16 GE	26 GE	8 CA	21 CA	5 LE	20 LE	4 VI	18 VI	1 LI

2043

	Jan.	Feb.	Mar.	Apr.	May	June	July	Aug.	Sep.	Oct.	Nov.	Dec.
Ceres	18 CP	0 AQ	11 AQ	22 AQ	2 PI	9 PI	12 PI	10 PI$_R$	4 PI$_R$	29 AQ$_R$	29 AQ	3 PI
Pallas	22 SA	5 CP	15 CP	24 CP	29 CP	29 CP$_R$	23 CP$_R$	15 CP$_R$	11 CP$_R$	13 CP	19 CP	27 CP
Juno	13 SA	23 SA	1 CP	7 CP	9 CP	6 CP$_R$	29 SA$_R$	24 SA$_R$	24 SA	28 SA	7 CP	17 CP
Vesta	13 LI	22 LI	27 LI	24 LI$_R$	17 LI$_R$	13 LI$_R$	16 LI	26 LI	8 SC	22 SC	8 SA	23 SA

2044

	Jan.	Feb.	Mar.	Apr.	May	June	July	Aug.	Sep.	Oct.	Nov.	Dec.
Ceres	12 PI	22 PI	3 AR	15 AR	27 AR	9 TA	20 TA	0 GE	8 GE	12 GE	10 GE$_R$	3 GE$_R$
Pallas	7 AQ	18 AQ	27 AQ	7 PI	16 PI	23 PI	27 PI	25 PI$_R$	19 PI$_R$	12 PI$_R$	8 PI	10 PI
Juno	29 CP	12 AQ	25 AQ	8 PI	22 PI	5 AR	16 AR	26 AR	2 TA	0 TA$_R$	23 AR$_R$	20 AR$_R$
Vesta	10 CP	26 CP	11 AQ	27 AQ	10 PI	23 PI	3 AR	9 AR	9 AR$_R$	2 AR$_R$	25 PI$_R$	25 PI

2045

	Jan.	Feb.	Mar.	Apr.	May	June	July	Aug.	Sep.	Oct.	Nov.	Dec.
Ceres	28 TA$_R$	28 TA	4 GE	13 GE	24 GE	7 CA	20 CA	4 LE	18 LE	1 VI	14 VI	25 VI
Pallas	16 PI	25 PI	5 AR	17 AR	29 AR	13 TA	26 TA	11 GE	25 GE	7 CA	17 CA	20 CA$_R$
Juno	26 AR	7 TA	21 TA	7 GE	23 GE	10 CA	25 CA	11 LE	26 LE	9 VI	22 VI	2 LI
Vesta	1 AR	11 AR	21 AR	4 TA	17 TA	1 GE	13 GE	24 GE	9 CA	19 CA	27 CA	1 LE

2046	Jan.	Feb.	Mar.	Apr.	May	June	July	Aug.	Sep.	Oct.	Nov.	Dec.
Ceres	3 LI	7 LI	4 LI_R	27 VI_R	23 VI_R	25 VI	3 LI	12 LI	24 LI	7 SC	20 SC	3 SA
Pallas	13 CA_R	5 CA_R	6 CA	15 CA	27 CA	11 LE	25 LE	9 VI	24 VI	7 LI	21 LI	5 SC
Juno	9 LI	12 LI	9 LI_R	1 LI_R	26 VI_R	26 VI	1 LI	9 LI	18 LI	28 LI	8 SC	19 SC
Vesta	28 CA_R	20 CA_R	16 CA_R	17 CA	24 CA	4 LE	17 LE	1 VI	16 VI	1 LI	17 LI	2 SC

2047	Jan.	Feb.	Mar.	Apr.	May	June	July	Aug.	Sep.	Oct.	Nov.	Dec.
Ceres	16 SA	28 SA	10 CP	16 CP	21 CP	21 CP_R	15 CP_R	9 CP_R	7 CP	11 CP	18 CP	27 CP
Pallas	17 SC	28 SC	6 SA	7 SA_R	3 SA_R	24 SC_R	18 SC_R	20 SC	27 SC	6 SA	17 SA	29 SA
Juno	29 SC	7 SA	14 SA	16 SA	13 SA_R	7 SA_R	1 SA_R	0 SC	3 SA	10 SA	19 SA	0 CP
Vesta	18 SC	3 SA	19 SA	26 SA	2 CP	1 CP_R	25 SA_R	20 SA_R	22 SA	0 CP	11 CP	23 CP

2048	Jan.	Feb.	Mar.	Apr.	May	June	July	Aug.	Sep.	Oct.	Nov.	Dec.
Ceres	9 AQ	21 AQ	2 PI	14 PI	25 PI	5 AR	12 AR	16 AR	15 AR_R	9 AR_R	3 AR_R	2 AR
Pallas	11 CP	23 CP	4 AQ	13 AQ	21 AQ	24 AQ	22 AQ_R	16 AQ_R	9 AQ_R	6 AQ	8 AQ	14 AQ
Juno	11 CP	23 CP	4 AQ	15 AQ	24 AQ	2 PI	5 PI	2 PI_R	25 AQ_R	20 AQ	22 AQ	0 PI
Vesta	9 AQ	24 AQ	9 PI	24 PI	8 AR	21 AR	3 TA	14 TA	21 TA	23 TA_R	19 TA_R	11 TA_R

2049	Jan.	Feb.	Mar.	Apr.	May	June	July	Aug.	Sep.	Oct.	Nov.	Dec.
Ceres	7 AR	15 AR	25 AR	6 TA	19 TA	1 GE	13 GE	26 GE	7 CA	16 CA	21 CA	21 CA_R
Pallas	22 AQ	2 PI	11 PI	21 PI	1 AR	10 AR	17 AR	21 AR	19 AR_R	13 AR_R	5 AR_R	1 AR
Juno	13 PI	26 PI	11 AR	29 AR	15 TA	4 GE	20 GE	8 CA	24 CA	9 LE	21 LE	0 VI
Vesta	8 TA	11 TA	18 TA	29 TA	10 GE	23 GE	6 CA	19 CA	3 LE	16 LE	28 LE	9 VI

2050	Jan.	Feb.	Mar.	Apr.	May	June	July	Aug.	Sep.	Oct.	Nov.	Dec.
Ceres	16 CA_R	12 CA_R	10 CA	14 CA	23 CA	4 LE	16 LE	29 LE	14 VI	28 VI	12 LI	25 LI
Pallas	5 AR	14 AR	25 AR	9 TA	25 TA	12 GE	0 CA	19 CA	7 LE	23 LE	9 VI	22 VI
Juno	3 VI_R	2 VI_R	26 LE_R	22 LE	24 LE	1 VI	10 VI	20 VI	1 LI	12 LI	24 LI	4 SC
Vesta	16 VI	17 VI_R	13 VI_R	5 VI_R	3 VI	8 VI	18 VI	0 LI	15 LI	0 SC	16 SC	3 SA

Lightning Source UK Ltd.
Milton Keynes UK
UKOW02f1351070616

275787UK00001B/73/P